Overcoming your Pharaoh!

Battling our issues, our instances, and our insecurities

Rev. Kelly R. Jackson

Overcoming Your Pharaoh!

Battling our issues, our instances, and our insecurities

ISBN: 978-1973969921

Contents

Acknowledgments

First of all, I give honor to my Lord and Savior Jesus Christ for giving me the strength through the Holy Spirit to endure until the end of this particular journey. This book has been a few years coming, with some divine detours along the way. However, I praise God for allowing to me to refocus when it was time and complete this project. To Him I give all glory and all honor. By His strength, which was made perfect in my weakness, I made it through.

Thank you to my amazing wife Angela for your continued sacrifices as I've gone further into the ministry. I realize that it's not always easy and I can be demanding, and I appreciate you standing by me through all of the ups and downs of ministry. God made you for me and I'm so very happy that you answered when He called. There's so much that I would struggle to do without you, and I appreciate you immensely for always being there.

To my son Kilen, Daddy's Big Man, I love you more than you will ever know. Thank you for making me smile when I'm frustrated, and thank you for giving me something to do when writer's block hits me. Your constant interruptions and need for snacks has helped daddy in ways that you'll never understand, and you probably don't care to. I see greatness in you, even as a 5 year old. Daddy loves you.

To my oldest son Steffen, I love you as well. Keep pressing toward the mark. I believe that you're figuring out life in your own way, much like I did at your age. I'm giving you the space to grow because somehow I know it's all going to work out just fine. Dad loves you.

To my Pastor and my super promoter, Damon Moseley, thank you for all that you've done for me spiritually, in ministry, in my printed work, and in all of the other areas of my life that you've stepped in. You are the epitome of a servant leader. Even in the midst of your own challenges, you've always found a way to be there for me. I couldn't ask for a better Pastor, but more than that, you are a true friend. I love you.

To Lady Dominique, thank you as well for your support and thank you for all of your inside jokes. Not a lot of people know the real you, and I think that's what I like about you. You don't need to be a part of any groups or cliques to still be you. I love you and I appreciate you.

To my Bethel Temple Church family, who so graciously got behind *Are We Still Making Disciples* and not only supported it, but followed along as we used it for Sunday School, I am forever indebted to you. From your support of my books to your support of my radio broadcast, you have embraced me with a true spirt of love and I will never forget it. Thank you from the bottom of my heart.

To my siblings and my extended family, I thank you for any and all support that you've given me in my various ministry endeavors. You are appreciated.

To the seniors at Brush Park Manor in the city of Detroit, my beloved Thursday afternoon Bible Class group, I love you all so much. It's such a blessing to be able to teach people each and every week that aren't trying to talk God out of being God. You all have been a blessing to my ministry and I just can't thank you enough for receiving me. You will always be in my heart, and you will always be on my calendar every Thursday at noon.

Last, but certainly not least, to my dear mother, Annie Jackson-Loritts. I never get tired of telling you how much I love and appreciate you. From the moments that you took care of me up until these current moments when I have to look after you, I have never gone a single minute without feeling your love. From the times you've called me up just to tell me that you believe in me, to the times that you've defended me against the attacks of others, I just want you to know that it never goes unnoticed or unappreciated. Thank you for being the best mother God has ever created. I'm praying that I've made you just as proud as you make me. I love you mama!

Kelly

Introduction

The story of Moses confronting Pharaoh is one of the most commonly told stories of The Bible. The idea for this book comes from Exodus Chapters 3 through 14, from Moses being called by God, to the Children of Israel being delivered by God. There's much to be learned from this entire ordeal (I encourage you to read it if you haven't and not just settle for the Hollywood version of the events). However, what our focus is on is not just the Israelites' deliverance from their captors, but rather it's on one man having to confront the captors in the name of regaining the freedom of a nation of people.

As you look through the story, you will see a man in Moses that revisionist history will often cause us to believe was always confident, always strong, and always brave. However, when you read your Bible, you see a man that lacked confidence, a man that had some physical limitations, a man that at times in his life exhibited questionable character, and a man that questioned God often about what he was being called to do. If you really get to know who Moses was, you find that he had his own personal Pharaohs to overcome before he could lead anyone else to freedom.

So, what exactly is a "Pharaoh"? In short, "Pharaoh" is a title for an Egyptian king or ruler. It is the Hebrew form of the

Egyptian title "the great house" (Source: The New Unger's Bible Dictionary). Just as it is with some of the titles we have today like President, Emperor or Prime Minister, the title itself doesn't necessarily mean oppression. Whether or not the people are being oppressed depends on the current holder of the title. However, for the purposes of our exercise and in line with our theme text, we are dealing with an oppressor.

Because of the story of Moses and the Israelites, we often equate the name or title of Pharaoh with oppression. Therefore, anytime someone seems to be in captivity, it reminds us of the most famous set of slaves in the history of mankind. Anytime anyone is dealing with any type of oppression, we think of the need for a great deliverer sent by God, just as Moses was.

However, just as the people had some physical bondage to break free from, Moses had some mental bondage to break free from. And even after leading the Israelites to freedom, it was revealed that they had developed a slave mentality. Many that have been enslaved by anything for a long period of time have no idea that they are being oppressed because they sometimes can't visibly see an overseer's whip. It's true in our lives in just about every facet. Our jobs, our relationships, yes, our churches, and even in our homes. We're often under oppression by the wiles of the enemy.

All bondage isn't physical and all chains aren't visible. Sometimes we're in bondage, and believe it or not, we're often co-signing the behavior through our refusal to confront our oppressors. We not only refuse to acknowledge what's going on, but when it's pointed out to us, we fail to acknowledge what's really happening to us. It was in fact stated by the great Harriet Tubman (who was referred to as "Black Moses" because she led so many Black salves to freedom) that she could've freed many more slaves had they only known that they were slaves.

And while we're there, let's look at the Black community as an example. Slavery is no longer in the cotton fields of the south, but rather in the board rooms of wall street and the admissions offices of institutions of higher learning that *sell* our kids their education without any guarantee of a job when they graduate.

We've copped to a slave mentality, and part of that slave mentality is not believing that the death of our young black men is a tragedy unless they're killed at the hands of a white police officer. It's not only a lack of awareness in who we really are, but also a lack of awareness of who God actually called us to be!

It's in us accepting behavior in our homes, churches, on our jobs and in our relationships that is beneath us, but acting as though we have no power to do anything about it. Our bondage begins mentally before it ever takes a hold of us physically, and in the end, if you keep a man mentally enslaved, it doesn't matter where his body is, he's still a slave.

Thus it was with Moses. Even though he had left Egypt 40 years earlier after killing an Egyptian and having a Pharaoh seeking to kill him for it, he was still mentally a slave because when you're always looking over your shoulder, you're in captivity. At one time, he was in the palace amongst royalty. By the time God called him, he was a runaway slave.

So here's a pressing question that must be answered: Can we be free if we don't know how? It's the slave mentality that causes us to adopt sinful behavior as "just how I am" and tell people that they have to deal with us as we are. If you've never been freed from the sin which doth so easily beset us, then you don't know that God has a better way, a better life, a better demeanor, a better attitude, and a better overall life for you.

Again, look at the Children of Israel that Moses is charged with confronting Pharaoh about. They had been enslaved for 430 years, and thus slavery was all they knew. Oppression and oppressors was all they knew. This group was born into slavery. Once you've been in bondage for so long, it's no longer bondage to you. It's life.

Some people are stuck in a rut because they chose the rut over the option of looking to God for a way out. So much so that even when the children of Israel got close to the

Promised Land, fear almost drove them back to Egypt because they felt safer in the "comfort" of their oppressor's land than they did in the wilderness with God. Imagine that. They felt lost without the chains that had them bound.

So, after 9 previous works, why is my face on the cover of *this* book? Believe it or not, this question came about after I was done with the writing of this book (I actually came back and added this explanation). The answer is, I'm overcoming something. I had to reflect on why it was there, and quite honestly, I said when I first started writing books that I would never appear on the cover. I wanted my books to be about the content, and not the cover.

If you have a copy of my first book, *Temporarily Disconnected* or its subsequent anniversary reissue, you'll see that the cover was basic and plain. Just a red cover and fonts. I wanted people to get the message, not the marketing. Little did I know, I was still branding it because it became known in many circles simply as "The Red Book".

By me putting my face on the cover of this book, I wasn't trying to promote me. I was overcoming my own personal stigma about being out front. I was exercising my faith in the fact that God wouldn't give me a message that could be overshadowed by me. I was stepping out of an insecurity that I had about being worthy to carry the message. I could never be worthy, but that doesn't mean that I should hide my face either.

Many may wonder why I look so stern on the picture. As one person put it, "If the book is about overcoming, shouldn't there be joy in your face?" Well, I believe in giving a true representation of the message. The truth of the matter is overcoming things in life doesn't always come with instant joy or immediate gratification. It comes with hard work, sacrifice, introspection, and sometimes a complete overhaul of who we are as people.

Overcoming can at times turn your life completely upside down. You may lose friends, family, money, and peace of mind along the way. And lest we fail to understand this point, overcoming Pharaoh is only the beginning! Once freed from bondage, we have the residue of bondage on us. Which means that Pharaoh is just one phase of getting our freedom.

There's still more to overcome. There's still a great challenge ahead. Forgive me, but that doesn't always cause us to smile, even though we're free. Sometimes, the smile doesn't come until later. Sometimes, your face represents your struggle. If we're really being honest and transparent, sometimes we look exactly like what we've been through.

I've always prided myself on writing in truth. Faith isn't a walk in the park. Faith is not always easy. Waiting on God to free you doesn't always come with a smile and a shout. It's hard. What you see on the cover is the face of a man that has survived when some odds were heavily stacked against him, and I still have some battles ahead of me. You see a man that has gone through much of the pain and strife that you'll find in these pages. A smiling face would've been disingenuous. There is truth in my face, because the struggle is real. But I assure you, there's joy in my heart because I'm a survivor.

As we journey through this book, it is my prayer that we can help you to identify what's holding you hostage. Not only that, it is our intent to get you to both identify and confront your Pharaoh. As Pharaoh faced 10 plagues from God during his resistance to Moses, we've covered 10 different Pharaohs in this book and given them names. Many of us remain trapped because we're in denial or we're afraid to call things as we see them. We're running to Midian just as Moses did, hoping things will blow over. But God didn't call us to be captives, even though sometimes He will *cause* us to be captives in an effort to get our attention.

Just as it was with Moses, God expects us to confront some things. Believe it or not, someone else's freedom may be tied to you confronting your fears. We can tell people that God is able, but it's much more powerful when they see it. It's important that we tell our problems about our God, but it's equally important that we deliver the message to the right address. Is your Pharaoh fear? Confront it. Is it sin or self-destruction? Confront it. Is it family or failure? Call it out! We can no longer afford to act as cowards concerning our condition. We must call it by name before we can be called out of slavery.

Prayerfully, no one reading this book is in any physical bondage, but in the event that you are, we hope to help you to break the mental chains of slavery so that when you become physically free, your mind can be free as well so that you don't wind up back in those chains.

For most of us, what's holding us hostage is the mental hold that sin and dysfunction often has on us. We have some barriers that we need to overcome in order to live as God has called us to. We hope to help you to identify Pharaoh, confront him, and break free. We hope to help you as you journey on to the place that God promised that you would dwell in.

As you go to confront Pharaoh, we dare not leave you without proper perspective. Getting out of bondage is never an easy proposition, even though getting there seemed to be. You can confront Pharaoh, but that doesn't mean that he will just lie down and let you go, and that fact isn't always the work of the enemy. Remember, it was God that hardened Pharaoh's heart. There are times when God will cause a problem just so that you can see His hand in the solution. There are times when God will send you into impossible situations just so that you can see what's possible when He's with you.

So I encourage you, as you read this book, exercise your faith. With God, all things are possible, but that doesn't mean that all things are easy. The things that oppress us are indeed powerful. Often more powerful than we realize, and that's probably why we tempt fate in the first place. However, there is no force greater than our God. No matter how long you've been in bondage, God is able to bring you out better than you were when you went in.

Be blessed.

Chapter 1

Pharaoh: Self-destruction

"What have I done to myself?" If you've never asked yourself that question, I would suggest that there's some denial somewhere in your life. No matter who you are, there's been a time or two in your life where things have gone wrong and you had no one to blame but yourself. We've all had those moments where there's been a self-inflicted wound here or there. Where this becomes an issue is when we pretend that someone else is at fault.

It's in our nature to pass the blame. Consider what happened in Eden. God gives a mandate and man disobeys. When God confronts him about it, man blames God (contrary to popular thought, Adam didn't blame Eve – Genesis 3:12 (NLT) "It was the woman YOU gave me who gave me the fruit, and I ate it"). From that moment on, we've been involved in self-destructive behavior. David and Bath-sheba. Samson and Delilah. Solomon and his many conquest, even after he asked God for wisdom. Self-destructive behavior is just a part of who we are.

As we look to overcome this particular Pharaoh in our lives, we can't focus so much on what's happening as much as we focus on our involvement. We often have a hand in some things that are happening in our lives, but we're just too proud to own up to it. If we could just stop ourselves, we'd find that a lot of the upside down things in our lives will start to turn right side up. I'm not in any way suggesting that you'll be trouble free, but wouldn't it be nice to look at the wrong in your life and know that you're just a participant, but not the cause?

Before we ever blame anyone for the troubles in our lives, we should ask the same question the Disciples asked at The Last Supper: "Lord, is it I?" That's a significant question because even though 11 of those men knew that they hadn't yet betrayed Jesus, when He said "One of you shall betray me", they almost seemed to understand that even though they hadn't done it, they were capable. If we could just come to the understanding that we're just as capable of harming ourselves as people are of harming us, we'd watch out for ourselves just as much as we watch out for others.

Consider these four thoughts:

1. Is the weapon in my hand?

One of the most popular and most quoted Bible Verses of all is Isaiah 54:17a (KJV): "No weapon that is formed against thee shall prosper". This is a verse that we usually use when we're under attack from our adversaries. However, we must always consider those times when our wounds are self-inflicted. Sure, there are enemy forces that rise against us, but what about those times when we were running with the devil? What about those times when Satan didn't force himself in, but rather we invited him in? What do we do when the weapon that was formed is in our hands and formed *by* our hands?

The general thinking in our lives is that any time something goes wrong, there's a force that's against us. While that's true in many, many cases, if we're being honest, there are times when we're actually against ourselves. There are times when we're involved in things that are detrimental to us. There are people, places, and things that we're readily available to, which causes much destruction to us. The weapon is formed, but it's our workmanship.

The reality is we can't continue to lament poor decisions when we're altering our state of being though intoxicants that hinder our ability to make sound judgments. We can't complain about backstabbers and people that are disloyal when we insist on hanging around people whose character and morals are suspect at best. We can't continue to wonder why God's most abundant blessings seem to allude us when we insist on alluding any type of sound and consistent Bible study beyond the preacher's sermon on Sunday morning.

So, consider some of these questions:

- How can we insist on being anything but godly in our dealings with our fellow man, while wondering why there's no loyalty being returned to us?

- How can we carry on in bad relationships with ungodly people, and yet wonder why God hasn't arranged a marriage for us?
- How are we expecting God to reward our unhealthy ways and habits with some of His best people? What kind of God would that be?
- Has success eluded you because you failed to match hustle, effort, and determination with all of the things you've prayed for?
- Are people blocking your dreams or are you unwilling to give attention to your calling?
- Before we yell "No weapon", we must ask ourselves, are we under attack or facing retaliation?
- What kind of people are we if weapons are continuously being formed against us?

These are tough questions to answer, I'm sure. However, sometimes, the most effective weapon the devil has against us *is* us. Again, we spend a lot of time watching out for people, but we often don't spend any time watching out for our own selves. Before we overcome everything else, the first thing we must overcome is us. We must make sure that we're not our own worst enemy. We can't continue blaming outside forces for an inside job.

As I've often taught, the devil will consistently present us with an alternative to God's Word, and he never comes with something that we don't like. He loads the weapon with things that our flesh can't resist. We must choose not to pick up the weapon. Is it true that we sometimes have unprovoked enemies? Absolutely. But we also must understand that God not only deals with actions, but He also deals with reactions. Meaning any weapon that is formed against you that wasn't provoked by you will not prosper, but you must also resist being a weapon of retaliation yourself.

Vengeance is God's and He will repay, but if you get in His business, He has to deal with your attacker *and* you. You can't put yourself in the crosshairs of God's righteous anger and then wonder why you're being punished. That being said, we must understand that the devil takes pleasure in our struggles, however they may come. We've got enough people taking shots at us. It'd be a shame if we're the ones giving them the ammo. It's an even greater shame if we're the ones forming the weapon and pulling the trigger.

2. "Sin lieth at the door…"

If we're going to overcome ourselves, that starts with monitoring our behavior. It starts with the understanding that sin is the thing that separates us from God and is at the root of all self-destructive behavior. It's a driving force for wrongdoing and it pushes us into some of our worst behavior. The fact that sin isn't preached as much as it used to be hasn't made it any less present or prevalent in our lives.

The statement "Sin lieth at the door" is found in Genesis Chapter 4 (KJV) during God's conversation with Cain. God tells Cain in Verse 7 that if He does well, he will be accepted and will be able to resist sin. However, if he doesn't, sin is waiting to overtake him. There was an ungodly attitude that Cain had that made him susceptible to evil, and eventually caused him to give in to it and kill his own brother. What we must remember is that sin is always on the other side of the door knocking. However, sin won't bust down the door. We have to let it in.

Understand that God is having the same conversation with us that He had with Cain. Is it always a life or death situation? Honestly, yes! It may not be a situation where we're going to kill our brother, but it could be a case of spiritual suicide if we're not careful. We can't open the door to sin, because once it gets in, there's no telling what we may wind up doing.

One major issue in the infiltration of sin into our lives is the assumption that we can control our sin. We assume that knowing a few scriptures or the fact that we're supposedly choosing sin, as opposed to sin overtaking us, is the same as being in control. We assume that sin didn't take up residence, but rather we allowed it to stay and we can evict it whenever we please. It's the same as believing that because we can swim, we're incapable of drowning.

Another issue that we have is the idea that the solo sin that we commit isn't a danger to us. We must understand that sin that only you and God knows about is still sin and must be addressed. God is not a silent co-signer in our wrong doing. We've got to be pleasing in His sight even when we're out of man's sight. Contrary to popular belief and conduct, we can't just quote our way to living right. There must be some application along the way. The Word must influence our actions and not just our emotions.

The Bible tells us in Psalms 119:11 to hide God's Word in our hearts so that we might not sin against Him. In Verse 105 of that same Psalm, the Bible tells us that God's Word is a lamp unto our feet and a light to our path. Nothing in the Word of God will turn your heart against God or lead you astray. Even when you're walking in some dark places, around some dark people, in danger of having some dark thoughts and committing some dark actions, it's the Word of God that will illuminate some better options for you. Sin lieth at the door. You've got to change your countenance. The best way to do that is by heeding the Word of God.

3. The Transparency Code

One of the new buzzwords in the church of today is "transparent". We like the idea of people, especially our leaders, bearing their souls and their issues for the benefit of encouragement. The thought behind this is that it makes us all seem a little more real, a little more comparable to one another, and it makes it seem as if we're all on a level field when it comes to sin and falling short.

The truth of the matter is if we wanted to know whether or not we were all in a similar place as it relates to sin, we didn't need to start leaning on the word "transparent". We just needed to open our Bibles and turn to Romans 3:23 (KJV): "For all have sinned, and come short of the glory of God". Sometimes, we're simply making things more complicated than they have to be.

For the sake of clarity, I want to be sure that it's understood that I'm not against being transparent. I think it's a great thing for our churches to be reminded that we all have our "something". This should encourage us to be more supportive of one another because we're all going through at some level. But I must remind you all that there was a time when people were consistently transparent in the church of old. It was called "Testimony Service". People would talk about their "whatever", and how God brought them out. The lack of transparency only came to the church when some of us outlawed testimonies because they made the services too lengthy.

However, there is an issue with being transparent these days. While it was a good thing to showcase that we all have our frailties, rather than being something that we're working on, it's now become a place where we stay. "Transparent" has now become code for "justification". Many of us aren't being transparent with a thought towards helping others that might be dealing with what we're dealing with. For some of us, being transparent is just a way to tell you what we've been up to willfully.

The Transparency Code is now sort of a preemptive strike. It's not necessarily a way to tell you our struggles so that you can avoid them in your own life, but rather it's a way to tell you what our habits are, just in case you catch us doing them. It's become a segue into telling people not to judge us when they catch us not doing better, even though we know better.

Where this harms us is when repentance goes missing. There's a difference between sharing your frailties, and rejoicing in them because you don't plan to change. Paul's statement that he will take pleasure in his infirmities (2 Corinthians 12:10) isn't a statement of pride. It is in fact a statement of weakness. It's a statement that he makes after seeking God three times for help concerning his weakness (2 Corinthians 12:8-9). He wasn't being transparent and then throwing in the towel by saying "This is just who I am now". In his weakness, he found that God's grace was sufficient to cover his weaknesses.

No matter how transparent we want to be about our sin, it's still sin and it displeases God. It's a weakness. A messenger of Satan. What we're transparent about is our thorn. Now, just to be clear, Paul said that he sought God three times about removing that thorn from his flesh. If I may, from my perspective, those are just the three times he told us about. If you really want to be better and not just transparent, you never stop asking God to remove the thorn.

Being transparent without an eye towards transformation is the same as being on the broad road instead of the narrow road. It's another trick of the enemy to tell us that we can fall short without ever trying to stand tall. If you're not trying to be better than you were yesterday, something is lacking in your walk. If you're not careful, you'll surrender to the devil whispering in your ear "Everybody's doing it and God's grace is available". But just because we're saved doesn't mean that we get to misapply and misrepresent grace.

In some ways, the idea of transparency is causing us to feel more comfortable living outside of God's Word. We must overcome that thinking. The more comfortable we become at carrying sin, the more it erodes our very being. Be open to people about the fact that you're not perfect, but also be open to the fact that you need to change. Be willing to share your story in a moment of transparency, but be able to tell people what you're doing to correct yourself.

"God is working on me" is a blanket statement, and at times, a cop out. Tell people how He's doing it. Talk about the steps you're taking. If you're not taking any, then start doing so. The better we become at carrying sin, the better we become at disappointing God. Some things we shouldn't desire to do at an expert level.

The mere fact that Paul calls his problem a "thorn in my flesh" suggests that he's uncomfortable with his issues. If we really want to be transparent, we'd talk about the pain and discomfort that living beneath God's standard is causing us. If we really want to be transparent, we wouldn't take pride in the fact that sin has taken up residence in our lives. We would want people to know that we're seeking God concerning the thorn, as opposed to surrendering to it and learning to live with the pain. We shouldn't just want people to see us clearly, we should also want them to see a clear way out. If we really wanna be clear and contrite in our transparency, we shouldn't show our faults without showing The Father.

4. What if it's not the devil?

As mentioned before, we often look for someone to blame when things are going wrong in our lives. We assume that every weapon formed against us has someone else's fingerprints on it. Usually, the first person we blame is Satan himself. He's our main culprit. And while it's true that the devil has his hands in a lot of trouble that finds its way to us, one has to wonder if he sometimes gets a bad rap.

What do I mean when I say that? Well, I'm just a firm believer that the devil doesn't make us do anything, he simply gives us the idea. At some point, we choose to give in. That being said, the devil may train you, but eventually, he takes his hands off. There are times when we're doing things that the devil taught us, but he's long been off the scene. There's a lot of things that we're involved in that he simply introduced us to. We're carrying on the relationship by ourselves now.

There comes a point in our lives where we begin to do things on muscle memory. Meaning that we've been doing them for so long, it's a part of who we are. It's natural now. We come to a point where we're simply doing what we do and the devil isn't even talking to us about it anymore, mostly because he's got us hooked and we're now on autopilot.

I understand that we often want someone to blame, but that often starts in the mirror. Even if the devil told you to do something, you gave in. There comes a point when we must understand that we're exercising some choices. Even in our preaching and teaching now, we have to start holding one another accountable and eliminating excuses.

Whether we want to admit it or not, there's always an option to poor behavior. It may cause us to have to swallow our pride, it may be uncomfortable, and it may cause us to do without some things that our flesh desires. However, the consequences aren't the same. The unyielding truth is that when we come face to face with God and we're asked to give an account of how we lived our lives, "The devil made me do it" won't be a suitable answer.

It's true, Satan is capable of throwing your life into a tailspin. But his being capable doesn't always make him responsible. Just as we often take credit for the successes of our lives, we must learn to take blame for the failures. Understand what was just said: Take blame for the failures, not things that went wrong that were beyond your control. Sometimes, we're just failing to do better. If we're honest, we've actively sought after some failing behaviors, and the devil was nowhere around.

If we're telling the truth, the devil didn't make us stay in relationships with the wrong people, we wanted what we wanted. If we're keeping it real, after a while the devil didn't keep you from church, you stayed away. If we're really being transparent here, the devil didn't keep feeding you gossip or encourage you to keep lying on people. You're just comfortable where you are now.

After a while, the devil is no longer a participant in the harm we cause ourselves. But make no mistake about it, he finds joy in the fact that we learned so well and we never stopped practicing what we were taught. He'll gladly take the blame as long as we don't do any better.

Conclusion

Some years ago, I used to do roundtable discussions about love and relationships with a group of friends and associates.

One of the things I always said to them concerning the decisions they made was "Always think it through". I wanted them to consider the consequences of their actions before they did whatever they were thinking of doing. I wanted them to be in a mindset where they always asked themselves "Why am I doing this?" I was wise enough to know that thinking it through wouldn't necessarily stop poor decisions, but it would bring the consequences to the forefront.

It's wasn't like I had never thought things through and then gone ahead with poor decisions in my life. In fact, if I may be "transparent", it still happens to me from time to time. However, with prayer and discipline, I've gotten better at heeding God's instructions. But the point remains that even when we take our time and think things over, we're still capable of self-destruction and poor decisions.

The struggle that we have in this flesh is that even when we take the time to confront the consequences of our actions, we will sometimes still talk ourselves into doing wrong. It's not that we don't see the consequences, it's just that we convince ourselves that we can outrun them. We tell ourselves that we can outsmart them. We say that we'll cross that bridge when we get there, never having a plan if the bridge is out and we can't swim. When our flesh is weak, we will literally talk ourselves into dangerous waters, sometimes even convincing ourselves that we can handle the fallout.

If we intend to overcome our self-destructive nature, a nature we were born with, a nature that has been in existence since Eden, we're going to have to submit to a wiser voice than our own. We slip into self-destruction because we simply ignore the Spirit when it tells us to stop. We miss the mark because we yield to the flesh with its temporary gratification, while denying the peace that the Spirit offers through obedience and submission.

If we could simply learn to love our future selves then we can learn to control our right now selves. What that means is the decisions that we make in the right now affect ourselves in the future. So when we do things that please the flesh right now, we destroy ourselves in the future. We make it hard for ourselves in the future.

Many of us are still carrying some things right now because our past selves didn't heed warnings. We're carrying some things today because we misused grace and God had to take it away for a moment. It's understandable that the devil may have tricked you. Maybe you misunderstood the power of sin, thinking you could control the uncontrollable. You may have even learned to live with the pain of a thorn in your flesh, confusing transparency with a license to stay stuck in sin. But I encourage you to get out of that rut.

Sin is a condition, but it's treatable. It can tear you apart if you let it, but you don't have to. You don't have to continue destroying yourself because you believe that's what life is supposed to be. "Nobody's perfect" shouldn't be the battle cry that you use when discipline and accountability are upon you.

Self-love should always be at a premium. If you don't love you, then no one else will know how because you can't teach them what you don't know. What we do to ourselves hurts us far worse than what others do to us. I'm encouraging you all to put the weapon down. Don't dance with the devil. Be transparent, but open to transformation. And overcome sin by not even inviting it into your lives.

Chapter 2

Pharaoh: Your past

Before attempting to overcome the past, we must first come to understand the nuances of the past and how even the worst of our pasts can sometimes benefit us, as opposed to irreparably harming us. We must also understand that there are times when we're more victim than prisoner when it comes to our pasts.

It's a fact that there are people that never wanna let you forget where you came from, what you used to be, and all that. However, dealing with your past isn't so much a prison as it is a rehabilitation center. With some hard work and some introspection, it's something that we don't always have to be freed from as much as delivered from.

I know that the new thing is "forgetting the past" as opposed to facing it, but I would caution against that logic before completely understanding what forgetting means in a spiritual context. Understand that to forget in a spiritual context isn't erasing our memory. It is knowing where we've come from, but refusing to dwell on it. It is understanding that there is a past, but refusing to be trapped there.

It's leaving the past in the past after you've learned the lessons of the past. You know what you did and what you were, but instead of being a hostage to that, you instead celebrate God for that fact that you are a "used to be". There are times when it's actually a good thing to be a "has been".

The struggle is in not allowing our memories to turn into actions or reruns of what once was. Even as naysayers gather to remind you of what you used to do (as if you don't already know), you must resist the urge to repeat the behavior just because it's being repeated to you. One of the greatest weapons the enemy will use against us is in fact our memory. Not only will he remind us of what we used to be, but he'll remind us of how much "fun" we had doing it, how good it felt to do it, and how free we felt when we were doing it. What he doesn't bring to your remembrance are the consequences. That information comes from God.

If someone was hurt by the former you, the devil won't remind you of that. If there were some decisions that cost you some valuable relationships, the devil won't remind you of that. If there are some parts of your being that were forever scarred by your former ways, he won't even bring that up. If I may invoke a sports analogy here, the devil specializes in the highlight reel plays, not the final score. The truth of the matter is many of us can look back on some times in our lives with great fondness, but the only thing that really matters is whether or not we were winning, losing, or learning.

So let's take a look at four key steps to moving beyond our checkered pasts:

1. You can't overcome what you refuse to acknowledge

We often hear the phrase "God erased my past", and I suppose that's one way of trying to leave things behind. However, we must understand that just because something was erased doesn't mean it was never there. We have the ability to correct mistakes because of God's grace and the work of Christ on Calvary, but that's not a license for us to behave as if certain things didn't happen to us, by us, or because of us.

The truth remains that all of us are who we are because of what happened in the past. Whether good or bad, the imprint of the past is on you. If you're a good and upstanding citizen, more often than not, that is the results of past training and upbringing. If you have some no so great traits, maybe it's a lack of training showing itself. So it stands to reason that our pasts cannot be erased, but they can be something that we don't talk about, bring up or dwell on. To erase our pasts is to erase us, and that's not possible. Whether good or bad, you are evidence of your past. It can't be erased. It must be acknowledged.

Now, let's be clear. There's a difference between acknowledgment and dwelling. Even for positive purposes, it isn't good to dwell on the past. The past can be a tricky place in that there are many fond memories that we have, and not everything in the past is a bad thing. Some things were regretful, while other things were just a learning experience.

Either way, it's always dangerous to dwell on things that are behind us. Even the good times can hold you hostage to what once was, when your attention should be focused on what is now, and what's to come.

Dealing with your past is the best way to overcoming the negatives of your past. Just as it is with substance abuse, there must be an acknowledgement. You can't just seek to "erase" it. We must own up to what we were and what we did. Ownership gives us the power to get rid of it when we're done with it. Ownership gives us the power to decide just how long we plan to deal with it.

People often try and hurt us with our pasts by bringing up the worst that we've done when we're trying to do better, or even the best that we've done when we're going through a rough season. However, this only becomes effective when we try and run from, hide from, or "erase" (deny) our pasts. When you have come to accept what you were, the sting of someone else seeking to "expose" you is often nullified. When you have accepted the fact that your past is directly connected to your current place and even your future, you won't be in such a hurry to pretend that it never happened.

It takes a very special individual to always use our past as a motivation for us, and not an indictment of us. Those people usually understand God's grace. Those are the people that you need to keep in your circle. Those are the people that understand that past transgressions lead to today's progression. We all need to remember that God pulled all of us from some place where we didn't belong, and if the truth be told, there are times when God had to pull us from the same place multiple times before we finally learned not to go back anymore. In fact, if His grace doesn't abound daily, we could easily wind up right back there at any moment.

Consider your past in the same way that you would a resume or a job application. Most of us have had jobs that we didn't like, and some that we may not have even been proud of. But it was those jobs that gave us some sort of experience for the next job. Either we found out what kind of job we never want to have again, or we learned that working on the ground floor is often necessary in order to reach the top floor. Whatever the experience was that we gained prepared us for the next phase of our lives.

Potential employers look at that resume and they see the experience. They see a willingness to work through difficult situations. They see a willingness to do whatever it takes to survive and get better. They see someone that may have tried and failed at some things, but they didn't give up. They see someone with experience in the worst, so they may be better prepared for the best.

This is what leaving the past on your resume can get you. People don't wanna know what you tried to hide from, tried to run from, or tried to deny. They wanna know what you defeated. They wanna know what you overcame. They won't see it if you insist on erasing all of your hurdles.

2. You can't change what happened, so stop trying

When we've done wrong in our past, once we've acknowledged what we've done, we tend to want to make up for it. There is, however, a difference between making up for something and trying to change what happened. As we've already discussed not trying to erase the past, the same thing can be applied to trying to change it or rewrite it.

There's often nothing more infuriating than someone that's done you wrong trying to change the narrative. Facts are facts and you're not really apologetic if you're trying to convince someone that what happened didn't really happen. The same is true with our pasts.

I get it. There are times when we look back and we cringe at what we once were. Sometimes there are things that are behind us that are so shameful that acknowledging what we did or what we were is just too painful. This is what causes us to look for that heavenly eraser and say "Lord, please make *that* go away". But the reality is the reality! You can't change it. It's there. It happened. And because we often do wrong with other people, there's a witness somewhere.

As we struggle with the details of the past, we mustn't try and change them, lie about them, sugar coat them, or even involve ourselves in a bit of revisionist history by changing their meaning or impact. Part of getting over the past is embracing what happened. Not in a sense of joy, but in a sense of acceptance, responsibility and accountability.

Don't try to rewrite it or reimagine it to try and make yourself look better or justify what you did. There may in fact be understandable reasons for why we did what we did, but if we're seeking a cure for a past that's holding us hostage, we must be honest about both the origin of the illness and the symptoms that were the results of it.

The saying goes: "Those that don't learn from history are doomed to repeat it". We can't seek to soften a blow that's already been landed, lest we end up throwing that same punch again. Whatever we've done in our past to hurt others or just ourselves, we've got to face it. We're living in a new day and age where we're repeatedly encouraged to let some stuff go, and that's good advice. But if we try to change what it is we're letting go of, the true facts of the matter may come back to haunt us.

True healing doesn't come from denial. Again, put the eraser down, and even more, put down the pencil that you've sought to use in order to rewrite an unpleasant chapter in life. Instead, read each paragraph and learn from its content. That thing that you said? It really happened! That thing that you did or were a part of? It really went down that way! It may be embarrassing, it may be hurtful, it may even be traumatic and catastrophic, but trying to alter the facts isn't even close to being the best way of getting over it.

3. Be willing to forgive yourself before asking anyone else to

Probably the most difficult thing in dealing with our pasts is the aspect of forgiveness. While we sometimes understand the need for forgiveness, we're often reluctant to go through the process of forgiveness. I've often found that this is due to a lack of understanding of what true forgiveness is. It isn't about acting as if it never happened (see previous section), but it is in fact an acknowledgement of what happened, the damage it caused, the fact that someone was hurt or wronged, and a spirit of true contrition.

True forgiveness doesn't always completely remove the scar, but it does treat the wound. Maybe it goes away, and maybe it doesn't. Some scars from certain wounds are forever. But when healing takes place, you may have the scar as a reminder of what happened, but you no longer feel the pain. Someone may notice your scar (a changed relationship) and ask you what happened, and while you remember what happened and can tell the story, you don't feel the pain anymore because you're healed.

In fact, there may even be some scars on us where we can't even recall the story of how they got there. And yet, you're healed. That's what forgiveness is. It's a healing. The scab is gone. The blood has stopped. There may be some scar tissue there, but believe it or not, that place on your body will sometimes heal so well, that it becomes stronger than places on your body that have never been hurt before.

When we're dealing with our pasts, we're dealing with some hurt and some pain that may be unresolved. Even if it happened long ago, there may be a scab, but no scar tissue. It may feel a little better, but there's no true healing as of yet. Before we can really move on, we must resolve this hurt. We must move from the ER to recovery.

However, what we often forget to do after we've asked for forgiveness is forgive ourselves. Some of us remain trapped by our pasts, not because others won't forgive us, but because we're so consumed with guilt that we can't forgive ourselves. But before we can get beyond the things of the past, we ourselves must be willing to let those things go. Not in a spirit of arrogance, but instead, in a spirit of true repentance.

Before we can even go to God for forgiveness, we must be willing to repent (meaning to turn away from our actions). We must come to Him with a mindset of never again going back to that place that caused us to be separated from Him. If you're going to ask God to let it go, you must be willing to let it go as well. If you're truly sorry for what you've done, you must be willing to forgive yourself.

This same principle applies to asking others to forgive us for past hurts. Again, not in a spirit of arrogance, but in a spirit of repentance. We must be willing to walk away from what we've done and leave it in the past. Not denying it, not erasing it, and not trying to change it. But instead, acknowledging it, owning it, apologizing for it, and seeking closure. In order to truly get past it, you've got to be willing to be done with it. Be willing to resist the desire to beat yourself up forever over something that you've repented for.

This mentality must be in place whether the person or persons you've wronged forgives you or not. Often times, we're stuck in the past or we're less willing to forgive ourselves because others are unwilling. Some people just aren't ready to let it go, while others refuse to let it go. Again, we must understand the requirements of forgiveness:

- Sincere repentance in your heart
- A willingness to openly admit wrong
- A willingness to take responsibility for your wrong
- A willingness to humble yourself and ask for forgiveness

You can't make a person accept any of these things from you. However, their unwillingness to accept them isn't your cross to bear. If they refuse to accept your sincere apology (and it must be sincere), then you've done all that you can do. Apologizing over and over isn't a requirement either, as such things are often done out of guilt. If you're sincerely repentant and it isn't received, don't hold yourself hostage to someone else's hostility. Be willing to forgive yourself. Be willing to heal.

Which brings us to our last point…

4. Get free: Don't be afraid to let go, even if others want to hold on

You can't hold on to your past because you're trying to hold on to certain people. You've got to be willing to let it go, even when others are holding on for dear life. Some of us are stuck in the past because we're stuck on some people. They're holding our pasts over our heads and we're allowing them to because we're trying to maintain the relationship. Living in history is never good for any of us.

If you really wanna be free of the past, you have the keys. Unlock the prison and walk right out. Don't be afraid. Don't be regretful. After you've done all that you can to move on from the past (see previous section), it's time to move forward. The only thing that you can gain from looking back is a testimony. Take the lessons learned and move forward with a better life and a better you.

There's no value in recycling past hurts and past issues in order to maintain current relationships. If people insist on holding on to the past as you're trying to move forward, that may be a sign that they belong in your past. Rehashing old issues, arguments, and incidents that have been resolved is not what a productive life consists of. Reopening old wounds time and time again is draining and counterproductive.

Some people only wanna talk about what was and what happened, but if we really wanna overcome such things, we need to put those conversations to rest. If we really wanna be done with what we say we're done with, we need to stop talking so much about things that we claim to be over. If we're done, we need to be done.

If you have people in your life that are in the history business, then it may be time for them to be history. You can't overcome the past with people that insist on living there. If you wanna move forward, you've gotta think forward. And sometimes, that requires being involved with a whole new set of people.

Conclusion: What is your testimony?

A testimony is about what happened, not what's happening! There's a difference between God bringing you through and God having brought you out. Both are definitely worth shouting about, but one is a process and the other is the completion of the process! If God in fact erased our pasts, then what kind of testimony could we possibly have?

In order to overcome the past, there must be evidence of a past. It had to have been there. We can't spend so much time trying to eliminate what God delivered us from. We shortchange God when we do that. While we don't have to place our past on a billboard for all to see, if no one else remembers where God brought us from, we should.

Also, let's be clear about what it really means to be transparent. Transparency can't just be a word that we substitute for justification. Some will share their struggles as a preemptive move, just in case you catch them falling short. That's not transparency, that's trickery. It's alright to be transparent as long as you're seeking a transformative word for your life (we discussed this in our chapter on self-destruction).

If we aren't transparent with a thought toward moving through our current issues, then we aren't helping anybody. People don't wanna know where you got stuck. They wanna know how you got through! Even when people refuse to let us forget, we shouldn't run from what we were. Our testimony should be a simple one: "I know what I was, but look at what I am now! God is amazing!"

Chapter 3

Pharaoh: Lack of support

The saying goes "Everybody needs somebody", but what do you do when you need "somebody" and "nobody" shows up? As someone that has gone into business for himself and pursued individual ministry, I could go on and on about how valuable the right support has been for me. It hasn't always come easy, nor has it come from places that I thought it should've come from. There have been surpluses and droughts, there have been ups and downs, I've had money and I've been broke, but one thing that has been a constant is the fact that God is faithful.

In the early stages of chasing your dreams, there's excitement, there are nerves, there's hope, and there's enthusiasm. As you're putting together all of your plans, you find yourself having enough energy to run through a wall. However, nothing saps that energy like finding out that you don't have the people behind you that you thought you would. Nothing kills your enthusiasm like people that will act like you're doing nothing at all. And nothing takes your nerves to the next level like that lack of support causing you to listen to the devil as he says "What if this doesn't work".

It's so easy to say the words "Step out on faith", but once you really have to, it can be a scary proposition. We say things like "As long as I've got Jesus", but if we're being honest, we often say that in a crowd of people that we expect to reassure us that we're not alone. I can't tell you how many times I wanted to stop. I can't tell you how many times I actually almost gave up on what God Himself promised me. I believed God. I just couldn't understand why the people around me wouldn't believe Him with me.

I had to come to understand, as you will too if you're in a similar position, that believing in God has nothing to do with trusting in man. Believing in God is a separate concept. It requires you to trust Him beyond what people will or won't do for you. In fact, the more people fail to support you, the more dependent you become on God.

You come to realize that you had your eyes in the wrong place. You come to realize that you trusted too many earthen vessels with the success of what God anointed you to do. You can count your family members, you can count your church members, you can count your friends, and you can count your acquaintances, but after a few no-shows at events and a few endeavors that went unsupported, you find out that as many as you can count, you can only truly count *on* God!

Before we get into the meat of this chapter, I do want to stress that we often have people around us that we expect to support us, and when the time comes, they actually do. They're right there at every event you sponsor, every attempt at ministry, and even just donating without asking for anything in return. However, when we're in the beginning stages of what we're doing, we often find out what we're lacking. Some people will say "Congrats", but never "How can I help?" Some people will ask "Where can I buy it?" with no plans to do so. People on social media will click "like" and "love", but never "Buy" and "Add to my shopping cart". And you still have to keep on.

The point here is that all of these things happen with our fellow man, but it isn't by God's design. More often than not, what God gives you is for the people around you first. However, it's always more difficult for home to get past what you used to be. They never saw you as CEO. They never saw you as Pastor. They never saw you as the answer to the family's financial prayers. Some families are so defeated by the devil that they struggle to believe that anything good can come from their lineage. They believe that success will only come from the outside.

Moses himself faced doubt and a lack of support from the very people that God sent him to lead to freedom, not only before the task was done, but even after. Consider the fact that Jesus Himself battled the same lack of support. His own family did not believe, save His mother (John 7:5). He had to use His gifts elsewhere, and the same may be true of you. But both Jesus and Moses had divine assignments, and so do you. A divine assignment calls for us to depend on the divine. Have you leaned on God as much as you have your own understanding of how this was supposed to go? Let's examine.

1. Did God promise you an earthly support system?

No matter what you do in life, you will need God in order to be successful. Philippians 4:19 tells us that God will "supply all of our needs according to His riches in glory through Christ Jesus". Those needs include your business needs, your personal needs, your family needs, your financial needs, and any other needs that you have. Our first dependence should always be on God and not man.

Now, to explain that further, we do often find ourselves relying on people for certain things, but where I believe we make our mistake is in the fact that we don't pray over our relationships like we should. Business relationships, family relationships, partnerships, volunteers, or whatever, we should be seeking God for His divine advice on who we should be connecting with.

The truth of the matter is we don't need people, we need God working through people. As we'll discuss in a couple of pages, those that we choose will often fall short of our expectations. However, when we allow God to fill out the roster, things tend to work a lot smoother.

God hasn't promised us that this person or that person would prosper us, because that's what He promised to do for us. The promises of man are finite and can only be filled through what God actually provided. Do you need earthly support? Yes, you do. But you need people that are divinely inspired and Holy Spirit led. Those are the people that God can do the most through. Those are the people that God will use in your endeavors when you follow His lead. Know that God never makes a promise that can only be kept by man.

Scripture tells us in 1 Corinthians 2:9 (NKJV): "But as it is written: 'Eye has not seen, nor ear heard, nor have entered into the heart of man the things which God has prepared for those who love Him'". Simply put, people that aren't connected to God or haven't contacted God through prayer concerning you will always have trouble accepting and supporting what God has called you to do. If they would just talk to God about you more than they talk to others about you, even if God doesn't show them the vision, He'll at least give them some peace about it.

2. Well-wishers vs. Supporters

There is some confusion about the difference between a well-wisher and a supporter. In fact, it's so confusing at times that even the people in these categories are confused about who they actually are. This is something that I definitely had to overcome as I went into both business and ministry for myself. These seem like the same group of people, but they're entirely different.

I believe where the confusion comes in is in the fact that more times than not, the people in these two camps actually love you. That fact is rarely in question. However, we've all been guilty of loving people, but not being there for them like we should have or could have at one point or another. And like marriage, we often assume that love is enough, when in fact, love is an action word and if you don't actively show love, you can come off as disingenuous.

When you're starting your business, chasing your dreams, getting a higher education, going into a relationship, or anything that requires outside support, you will need both supporters and well-wishers. And though they may be confused about who they are, it would do you well to know the difference. Knowing the difference can not only help you in terms of keeping your emotions in check, but it also helps you manage expectations.

So, here it is in a nutshell:

- **Well-wishers** – These are people that genuinely wish you well in your endeavors. When they tell you that they're praying for you or they hope you do well, they really mean it. They often care about you and want you to get whatever you're chasing. Don't sell them short because we all need love and prayers. They'll go as far as they're willing to go, and that's about it. They don't mean any harm, they're just not going above where they are.

- **Supporters** – Supporters are well-wishers, but with a lot more effort. Supporters are the ones that love you, pray for you, want you to do well, and will help you (both physically and financially) whenever and wherever they can. These are the people that will come to your event when no one else does, because they understand that being present when you're able to matters. They'll buy what you have, even if they don't need it. They'll promote wherever they can. They push and they encourage, as well as offer helpful feedback. These are the people that will do all that they can to help you succeed, even when the dream changes form here and there.

Now, let me be clear, we all have both of these traits in us. We all know some people that are doing some things that just isn't our thing. We wish them well, but we won't support financially or with our presence. And, let's be real, sometimes people that you love are doing things in some places that just isn't your scene. It's not your crowd, nor is it something you're passionate about. Sometimes the best that you can do is wish them well and there's nothing wrong with that.

Also, I must stress the difference between people that are genuine well-wishers and people that are just giving you lip service. Some people will say that they wish you well, but nothing could be further from the truth and they literally couldn't care less. I don't want these people confused with people that really do care whether or not you make it, but they aren't passionate enough to get behind it any further than they do.

What we must all understand is the difference. Don't claim to be a supporter when you've never sown into anything or gone to anything. Don't claim to be a supporter when you've had opportunities to do more than say "God bless you" or like a Facebook post about an upcoming event or a new business venture and you didn't do it. Support is more than words, its action. If you wanna move from well-wisher to supporter, you're gonna have to actually do something.

As for those that are chasing your calling in life, you must understand the difference as well. Don't expect well-wishers to do what a supporter would do. Don't sit around asking why certain people won't sow into you when the only thing they've ever done is pat you on the back. Those are well-wishers. Take it for what it is, because as I stated before, outside of financial backing and physical presence, you do still need love, prayers and people that wish you well.

Identifying these two groups of people will ultimately help us to manage our emotions as well. You won't be as angry or disappointed in people that don't support certain things when you know they're just a well-wisher, and you'll be pleasantly surprised when they go above and beyond. Conversely, you'll come to appreciate your supporters much more because you'll understand that they could be giving you much less.

3. Those who should often won't

If there is a ground zero for the Pharaoh that is lack of support, it is people that should be supporting you, but don't. It's true that those that are closest to us are often the first to know what we're doing. It would seem that nobody would be on board quicker than they are. Now, for some of us, this is the case, and if that's you, consider yourself blessed. However, the reality is that more times than not, there are people closest to you that should be backing what you do, but they just won't.

Now, I'd love to tell you that I'm gonna write something that will make you feel better about close support being hard to come by, but I'm sorry, that's just not the case. You may get a better understanding, but you probably won't feel better. You may get some clarity and you may even get closure, but you may not feel better about it at all.

The thing about the people that are closest to us, which is family, friends, co-workers, and fellow church members, is that they're often falling into that category of well-wishers. Which means that they aren't necessarily praying against your success, but they often won't do much to help you either. The fact is most of these people that are close to you believe that it's enough that they root for you. They don't feel the need to put much more effort behind you than that. When you're a kid, they attend everything. When you're an adult, it's hard to get on the schedule.

I've often stated to entrepreneurs or people that are starting out in ministry that family is just the first group of people to tell you no. Often, if they can't make money off of what you're doing or directly benefit in some other tangible way, they won't help. Not true in all families, but definitely true in a lot of them. Many family members are often the first group of freeloaders and hangers on that you'll meet, when they should actually be the ones paying full price to help you get started.

There's something about our families (and I must be honest, this is definitely true in the Black community) that feels as if they're owed something because they're related to you. Because they watched you grow up, babysat you, changed your diapers, or whatever, they somehow believe that your dreams don't take finance. They somehow believe that nostalgia is currency or money for overhead. The people that should be responsible for your startup are often the ones that wanna put you in the hole right out of the gate.

Some friends, just like family, will always want a sample of what you're doing, without ever coming back and paying full price for the whole thing. Where they should be helping you on the ground floor, they're treating you like you've already made it to the top and have much to spare. These friends and family should be investing in you like supporters, but instead, they're like well-wishers, staying just far enough away to not have to commit, but just close enough to say "I was always there", just in case you actually do make it.

What's always amazed me is the fact that we'll go to our favorite department store and buy the products of strangers without a second thought because it's in the stores, and therefore, we trust it. We disregard all of the trial and error that the inventor had to go through in order to get to that store. We disregard all of the support that it took for that person to make it.

Now, while much of what's been said is related to business, this is much more prevalent for those that pursue ministry in one form or another. I once said on my radio broadcast that some people won't support you *because* you're in ministry. Meaning that they will use the fact that you're depending on God against you. They will use your faith as a way to withhold their support, reminding you of what you say you believe: "God will provide".

They don't accept the fact that God provides, but He uses the people that are down here. God's way of providing is giving us the means to help those around us that are trying to make something of themselves, and the people that claim to love them should be willing to go much further than strangers on the street. I understand not supporting something that you don't believe in or have faith in, but when you can see a call on someone's life and you still won't support because "that ain't nobody but (insert childhood nickname)", then it's no longer about the individual and all about you.

In ministry, it is much more difficult to garner support because when ministry is done properly, it's not about a product as much as it is about a calling. Supporting ministry requires a level of discernment that many around us just haven't tapped into. While people will buy a product based on advertisement and word of mouth, discernment requires something deeper. Discernment will tell you more than word of mouth ever could.

People will always struggle to put their money or their presence behind a "calling". There's been many a preacher that didn't get the support of those close to them until they actually became a pastor, and sometimes years beyond that, even though the call had been on their lives for years and years. There's been many a church lead singer that didn't get the support of the church they grew up in until they were somewhere recording their first gospel album. What God has whispered in the ears of many often goes unsupported by those close enough to have heard the whisper, but it's embraced by people that first heard it through a megaphone.

Again, the prayers of well-wishers are valuable and needed. However, it's frustrating to have people telling you to follow your heart and chase your dreams, but never be willing to lend the actual support that's needed to do so. It's frustrating to hear people openly express doubt as you were chasing your dream, only to see it taking form, and they still refuse to get on board because they can't admit they were wrong. And it's so very discouraging to see people go everywhere else and spend more money on strangers that do the very same thing that you do, while never giving you a chance to share your gift without asking for a discount.

Understand that some people wish they could do more, but can't. Those aren't the people we're talking about here. But what we are discussing are people that will rave in social circles and on social media about a big chain retailer when a family member just opened a boutique. I'm talking about people that will support a big chain restaurant, but won't support a friend's food truck, but will still go to that friend's free cookout at the house. This is about people that can, but won't, and will still tell you that it's all love.

4. The Source vs. The resource

As we sort through who will and won't support, we must remember to always keep our focus on where our help comes from. It's still true that all of our help comes from The Lord, and He shows up in many different forms. As people have told you that "God will provide", whether they were speaking their true feelings or just brushing you off, there's still truth in the statement. God will provide!

If there's anything that we can learn from a lack of support, it is to trust The Source more than we do the resource. While a resource is something that we can draw on, the source is where things originate. We keep going back to Psalms 24:1: "The Earth is the Lord's and the fullness thereof. The world and they that dwell therein". Consider that in conjunction with Genesis 1:1: "In the beginning God created the Heaven and the earth". What that means is that the earth belonging to God didn't come to be by inheritance. He created it. It's His. This world and everything in it!

As we look here, there, and everywhere, we must first look to The Source of all things. We must look to the place from which everything comes. It's so easy to get caught up in who didn't, who should've, and who won't, that we forget who can and who will.

If we're really clear about this, God has a way of making those that fell short come full circle and get behind you. Not only that, we must remember that God will bring support from some unlikely places. There are people out there right now that you were convinced would never do anything for you, and God intends to use them to boost you to greater heights.

We must remember that the people that God has placed here are simply resources to be used, but He is in fact The Source. The level of support that we receive is determined by God. Your marketing plan matters, your presentation matters, your professionalism and your skill matters, but none of that matters more than the God that gave you all of those things.

Conclusion

Before seeking the support of anyone, ask God to guide you to your supporters and to help you to appreciate your well-wishers. When you recognize that all of your help does come from God, you also realize that you're never lacking, you're sometimes just looking in the wrong places.

Every time that God's gives us gifts and talents, they come with a promise. There isn't anything that God has given us that won't prosper us. Understand that prosperity doesn't always mean an overwhelming abundance of money, but it does mean that you will succeed if you just trust Him.

He has a way of putting you in the way of success, around people that will assist, and in the places that will most benefit you. The Bible tells us in Proverbs 18:16 (NLT) that a man's gift can open doors for him and gives access to important people. That means that the gift that God gave you is its own support as well. It means that God will provide *through* your gifts. It's not that the people that you were counting on weren't important at all, but they weren't important at this stage of you developing in your purpose.

Down the line, all of the people that looked the other way as you climbed the mountain will have to take notice because you'll be standing on top of that mountain. Some people just aren't made to support a dream, much less dream for themselves. God has given you something to look forward to, and at times, it's so far down the line that even you have to squint to see it. You can't lose hope over people that can't see past the hurdles.

Consider the fact that Moses had to lead a people to a Promised Land that not even he had ever seen. As they journeyed through the wilderness, some lost faith and hope. Even after spies were sent out to scout the land, only two brought back a good report despite some obvious challenges (because they trusted God more than they feared the challenge), and yet some still wanted to go back to captivity because they thought they were better off there (Numbers Ch. 13 and 14).

What that means for you and I is some people won't support you even when there are two or three that can see the possibilities in what you're doing. Don't be discouraged! As you chase after what God has put in front of you, don't despise those that lack the faith and courage to get behind you. They weren't there when God told you. They weren't there when God showed you. They may even still believe that God is able, they just didn't know He was gonna choose you. Don't be bitter. Don't be angry. And by all means, don't give up. Show them better than you tell them.

Chapter 4

Pharaoh: Self-doubt

Nothing can stop us like our own insecurities can. It doesn't matter whether the insecurities are of your own making or if they're put on you by someone else, if you don't have the right confidence, there's a lot that you won't be able to get done in life. It's true that real success begins in the mind, and if you are the type of person that doubts yourself, then you're constantly afraid to pull the trigger on some things that God is just waiting to bless.

One of the things that increases our feelings of doubt is God putting some incredible dreams into our feeble minds. God will show us some things that are so large and so elaborate, that we tremble more out of fear than we do out of anticipation. The crazy thing about what God does is that He sometimes taps into our inner most desires, things that we didn't even realize we wanted to pursue. He'll literally prepare us for the desires of our hearts, and it scares us.

In our flesh, we'll sometimes get so wrapped up in the dream, the vision, or the task, that we forget who's orchestrating it all. We forget that God is the one that gave us the inkling to do whatever it is that we're passionate about. We forget that God, as our Father, is responsible for His children. He makes the promise, and He always delivers.

You received the call of God, and He's not about to allow you to carry this vision on your own.

Our doubts are often a result of a lack of vision. It's also the result of us wanting everything to be easy and simplistic. Our fear of challenges or our inability to see what God has promised above any obstacles is also a hindrance. The first time the bank denies a loan, we wanna give up on the promise. The first time we can't get everyone on board with the vision and we realize that we'll have to get it off the ground alone, we wanna throw in the towel. The first time the first try isn't successful, we begin to doubt if anything that we've been chasing is real.

What we can't ever afford to do is allow the God of the promise to get lost in our doubts. I contend that doubts are never of God. If you're in the wrong place, God won't fill your head with a doubt that you can find a way to rationalize. If you're in the wrong place, God will just tell you to stop or He'll tear down what you're doing. As we go forward into this chapter, there are some things that I want you to consider. These are just a few critical points to understand so that you might get past your doubts, and on to your destiny.

1. It's not by the power of your might

Something that I've been stating in my teaching and in my writings over the last 5 plus years is this: Never put your limitations on God. What that simply means is just because you can't see how it can be accomplished doesn't mean that it can't be done. God is beyond man's limitations, and therefore He can do exceedingly, abundantly above all that we ask for, and He doesn't need our help to do it.

It's definitely a good thing for us to be aware of our limitations, but it's also important that we be aware that God never gives us an assignment that He expects us to do all alone. I know that there's a mentality that God expects us to do certain things ourselves, but the reality is we never do anything ourselves. If God doesn't replace the next breath that we take, we're outta here. We need to always be aware of the fact that God is involved in the major parts of our lives, as well as the minuscule.

When I come to understand that God is indeed involved in all aspects of my life, I can also come to a place where I see that I'm dependent on Him for literally everything. Knowing that I can't even live by the power of my own might, I'm even more aware that I can't do anything else just based on my own strength. The Word of God tells us in Acts 17:28 that it is in Him that we live, move, and have our being. That Verse illustrates that God is the very life living inside of us. We are powerless to do anything without His involvement.

Therefore, whatever assignment we may be under, whatever gifts and talents we've been given, whatever anointing we may be walking in, it all starts with the life that we've been blessed with. It all starts with God deciding to wake us up each and every morning. As much as you may doubt yourself from time to time, the mere fact that you have a God that's keeping you from day to day should cause you to never doubt Him.

When people are questioning how it is that you're doing what you're doing, you can start by telling them that your rising each day isn't even of your own accord, and therefore, whatever it is that God is allowing you to do, you're simply a conduit and a vessel through which He's working. Which leads me to my next point…

2. You didn't choose you for this assignment

So many of us fall into a place of self-doubt because we don't quite understand why God chose us to do what we do. And that right there is a key statement: God chose us. We didn't go shopping for gifts and talents. God developed that in us. Even for those of us that operate in our gifts at a genius level, rest assured that there's something on this earth that we'd fail miserably at if we tried. Nobody does everything great. We all have deficiencies somewhere.

As we go forward and walk in our gifts, doubt will creep in on some of us because we sometimes believe others to be more deserving or more fitting for whatever it is that we're doing. What's even more challenging for us is when we see someone walking in a calling similar to ours, and they seem to be excelling in ways that we aren't. If we're not careful, self-doubt can easily turn into jealousy, and before we know it, we're no longer walking in the <u>authenticity</u> of the call, but rather we're walking in what we think the call should look like.

The key is, not only has God chosen whom He's chosen for whatever call it may be, but He's also determined how they should do it. We can't allow ourselves to doubt God because we're doubting ourselves. We didn't choose ourselves, we didn't choose the path, and we didn't choose the style in which any of this should be done, and I believe it to be a disrespect to God to try and change any of it.

It's also easy for us to start listening to outside voices that will remind us that what we're doing doesn't look like what others are doing, or even how our predecessors did it. For example, this kind of thing rears its head in preaching a lot. Certain people are used to a certain style of preaching, so much so, that if they see people that don't do it the way they're used to it, they assume it's not authentic.

This is dangerous territory because this is a place where our haters will actually have our undivided attention. I know it's fashionable to pretend that haters never get our time or our attention, but if we ever plan to overcome haters, we must acknowledge the fact that sometimes their thoughts and opinions have us bound. If we ever plan to break the bonds of a hater, we must accept the fact that we not only sometimes listen to them, but we also adjust to please them.

There is no call that you can be under that the devil will be pleased with, and he will dispatch his agents to give you hell at every turn. Yes, I know that you're walking in what God told you to, but you're not strong enough to make the devil quit his job. He will come for you, even though you're chosen of God, and sometimes, *especially* because you're chosen of God. And make no mistake about it, if God hasn't designed you for this, you will crumble under that pressure.

Consider the theme of this book once again. Pharaoh didn't care that the Children of Israel were God's chosen people, nor did he care about Moses' supposed authority. Not only did he resist, but he sought to intensify the captivity. So therefore, we must understand that not everyone is for us. No matter what you're anointed for, no matter what you're called to, no matter what your skills or gifts are, some people are gonna be against you "just because".

Not everyone is for you, but that's not all bad. If you want to know the truth, there are some people that should never be on your side because truthfully, they're not on God's side. If everyone is against you, that should concern you because God will always give you some support, but there are some people that are just opposed to the things of God, no matter what the evidence says, and it will take an act of God to change their hearts.

Here's the shouting good news, though: Romans 8:31 reminds us that if God is for us, who can be against us? Now, let's be clear and give you some context. That statement doesn't suggest that no one will ever rise against us just because God is for us. That statement is a reminder that they will not prevail against us.

Understand that some opposition is good for us. In fact, some of it is God-ordered. Remember, Scripture tells us that it was God that hardened Pharaoh's heart. God wants to make sure that He gets the glory for what He's going to manifest in you, even in the face of haters and opposition. God placed the call on your life. It was your job to answer, even if those around you disagree.

3. What you have is what you need

Let's go back to how it is that God expects us to administer our gifts. I want to be clear about the fact that there's nothing wrong with training. In fact, it's encouraged. I've had many great mentors in my life, from pastors, friends in the ministry and my mother. In addition to that, I've had some schooling. There's nothing wrong with honing and enhancing your skills. Just be sure that you're seeking edification and enhancement for the Kingdom's sake, and not just for personal gain.

God will place some raw talent in us that often needs to be developed. What we must guard against is changing the nature of the gift. Again, enhancement is one thing, but attempting to change what God gave you is something entirely different. God has already placed the seed inside you. Your job is to nurture and grow it, not rip it from the ground.

Many of us will try and change or alter our gifts because we have our own ideas of what it should look like. Look at Moses once again. He had a preconceived notion of what a leader of God's people should be and sound like, and it was all external. God was looking at Moses' character. He was looking at his heart and his love for his people. God knew what he had placed inside of Moses. He needed courage. He needed a mouthpiece. What he didn't need was to try and change who and what God had made him. He just needed some enhancements that only confronting Pharaoh and the subsequent challenges of leading the Children of Israel would bring him.

We will often wonder why God didn't give us certain skills or abilities, and we'll wonder about that because those skills are what we desire to have. Let's be clear, God will allow us to have some external gifts or some additional talents if we desire, but the goal should never be to replace what God calls for with what we desire. Some of the things that we want to do are outside of the lane that God called us to be in. There may come a season for that at some point in our lives, but we must wait for that season. We must administer our gifts the way that God called us to, lest He come and take them away.

If we accept the fact that God has given us what we need for the task at hand, we will find satisfaction in serving Him. That doesn't mean that God won't allow other things to flourish at other times in our lives, but we must stay in step and in season with God until He decides it's time for a shift. Being what God called us to be should always be of greater pleasure than being what we want to be or what we believe our call should look like.

Know that God doesn't choose like we choose. He chooses based on the inside of a man. The Bible tells us that we are His workmanship (Ephesians 2:10), therefore, He puts inside of us exactly what we need to complete the task before us. Even if it's just a seed that needs to be developed, there is much power in that seed. Man may not always see what's growing and developing inside of you, but God does.

4. All means all!

For the sake of quoting, Philippians 4:13 is one of our favorite Bible verses: "I can do all things through Christ who strengthens me (NKJV)". However, we're often out of context. We use it in relation to getting jobs, getting material possessions, and so forth. While God can get in all of those things and work it out for you, context matters.

Paul was making this statement while in prison, where death could've come at a moment's notice. In a place of desperation, he still had his hope in God. Even in that situation, Paul knew that God was the God of that circumstance as well, and He could deliver him if He so chose to. For that reason, Paul was confident that he could endure!

I once preached "The Blessing In All Things" from this very text. I stressed the fact that the word "all" was in fact all inclusive. It included everything. Nothing was left out. While we may not find ourselves in the same type of prison that Paul was in, where our lives are hanging in the balance, we must understand that self-doubt can be a type of prison. You can't serve God and operate in your gift if you're trapped by "what ifs" and all manner of doubt. You must embrace the idea that you can do it all through Christ, and all means all.

While some people are quick to tell you what they think they're anointed for, in reality, a call from God is often frightening. If you want to know the truth, it scares the hell out of us because we're often on our way to hell when God calls us, just as Paul was before God changed him. It's not just that we *feel* ill-equipped, we actually are. There's some work that must be done on us before the real work can begin through us.

If a call from God doesn't at some point feel overwhelming to you, I question whether or not you've been called. If you didn't have a conversation with God similar to the one that Moses had when he got the call, you may be chasing your own calling or the calling of someone else. When God calls you, it's often such a departure from what you planned for your life or what you believe yourself to be capable of, you might literally become paralyzed with fear.

All of these feelings are valid and understandable. They're even applicable, if you plan on doing things according to your own strength and your own capabilities. But if you're planning on following in Paul's footsteps and doing it all through Christ, I submit to you that you can make it. God won't call you and then leave you. God won't empower you without enabling you. And God won't allow you to fail at what He created you to do. You can do it all through Christ. And all means all!

Conclusion

Doubt is what will kill our dreams before anything else will. Before failure, before haters, before people trying to roadblock us, even before the devil. If you're defeated in your own mind, you won't ever need enemies because that job will already be taken by you. If you've convinced yourself not to go, no one else has to get involved. You have accepted the terms of defeat.

I know, somewhere in your mind, you may find yourself thinking that the safe thing to do is to never risk anything. Well, that's the talk of people that have already failed. The tragedy in that is failure is a part of life, but there's a difference between a failed endeavor and a failed life. Successful people have failed endeavors on the road to success. Failures never left home, so they don't even know what the road to success looks like.

If we don't get anything else out of this chapter on self-doubt, we should get that self is a part of the equation. Self can stop you from doing some incredible and amazing things. Self can talk you out of more things than anyone else can, mostly because more than likely, you trust yourself more than you trust anyone else. So when *you* are telling *you* that it won't work, *you* believe every word you're saying.

Even when it comes to others talking you out of your destiny, it takes self to listen. When people are putting their doubt into your head, it doesn't become yours until you accept it and buy in. Self-doubt doesn't happen without your involvement, and we must learn to check ourselves before we ever try and check anyone else. I know what they said to you, but what did you buy into?

Most importantly, self-doubt will talk you out of the simple, but powerful fact that God is indeed able. As we've gone through this chapter, there's once central theme: Wherever we lack, God fills in the blanks. It's human nature to doubt yourself at times, and for that reason, you can't rely on your human nature when dealing with a spiritual God concerning a spiritual calling.

Consider 1 Corinthians 2:10-16, which reminds us that God reveals things through His Spirit to those of us that are indeed spiritual. To the natural man, what God has promised is often foolishness in his eyes. The natural man will always struggle with the promises of a spiritual God. Therefore, doubt is contradictory to who we clam to be. If we claim to be spiritual, then we must operate in the spirit, which is faith, and not the flesh, which is doubt.

As Moses went back and forth with God, the conversation shifted from how God would equip him, to how God is in fact God. Moses struggled to accept that God would equip him, so he had to be convinced that God is more than capable just on His own. This is how we can overcome self-doubt and hesitation as it relates to the promises of God. Whenever you can't, He can. When you're unsure, He is your reassurance. Whenever you can't see, He'll give you the vision. Move self out of the way, and watch God make a way.

Chapter 5

Pharaoh: Fear

One of the biggest misconceptions that we have is that you have to be a coward in order to be afraid. There is a major difference between cowardice and people that are afraid of certain things in life. For example, people that fear death may not fear anything else in life. But the inevitable, that one thing that no man can control or stop, may be that something that causes them great fear.

Considering the fact that we all have dreams and aspirations in life, fear becomes a topic of conversation often because so many of us fail to live out what we aspire to. That failure doesn't always happen because of cowardice. It sometimes happens because of uncertainty. It happens because of the unknown. It happens because we're afraid to fail (we'll cover that in the next chapter). We often fail to live out our dreams because we want guarantees that life just doesn't provide.

For us Bible students, we know that it's the devil that causes us to fear. When God gives us talent, ideas, business plans, aspirations for enterprises, or entrepreneurial dreams, it's the devil that comes along and whispers in our ears "That's impossible" and "You can't do THAT". When God tells us to leave our comfort zone and do some things that nobody will understand, it's the devil that will cause us to pause by asking us one simple question: Are you sure God said that?

I know we like to quote Philippians 4:13 and tell the devil "I can do all things through Christ", but don't you know that the devil isn't afraid of you? I know you've got mustard seed faith, but don't you realize that faith that isn't challenged isn't really faith? We can't continue on thinking the devil is a wimp concerning us when he's not. He may be a thief. He may be a liar. But he's certainly not afraid of us! He will challenge us! But he's no match for God and no match for God's Word.

So how can we break free from the paralysis of fear? How can we break away from that thing that consistently tells us that we can't, even as God says we can? Let's examine some tools that we can use to conquer fear.

1. Stay in touch with the Spirit that God gave you

2 Timothy 1:7 clearly states that God didn't give us a spirit of fear, but that doesn't mean that we don't still have access to that spirit. In relation to the text, Paul was telling Timothy to be courageous and bold in his ministry, but to also be loving and to operate in wisdom. While Paul was speaking to Timothy concerning his preaching and pastoral ministry, we must not assume that this Scripture has no meaning for the layperson. If we are in fact saved, our lives are a ministry,

and therefore, whatever we do should not only be done to the glory of God, but we should also do it according to the Spirit that God has placed inside of us.

Proverbs 4:7 tells us that wisdom is the principle thing, and therefore, we should get wisdom because it leads to understanding. I believe that the reason some of us operate in fear is because we lack wisdom. Not necessarily about the circumstances, but about God. I wrote in my book *An Understanding with God* that some of us know God, while others simply know *of* God. If you plan to go boldly after your goals and dreams in life, you have to come to understand just how powerful God is, even in the face of your limitations.

The theme for this book is dealing with Moses confronting Pharaoh. During the time that God is telling Moses what He wants him to do, Moses is outlining his own limitations. Partly because the task is daunting, and partly out of fear. With you being Moses, and whatever you're seeking to accomplish being your Pharaoh, you have to have a certain level of wisdom about God. If what God is telling you to do seems impossible, you have to understand how an all-powerful God can enable you to overcome whatever obstacles are in front of you.

As it relates to our human fears, God has already provided a solution to that. Every doubtful "what if" that exists in your fleshly spirit has been eliminated by a supernatural spirit that

God has placed inside of you. So if God has called you to something, not only will He see you through it, but it's also His responsibility. Yes, once God calls you, you're not only obligated to Him, but He's also obligated to you!

Scripture tells us that God is not a man that He should lie (Numbers 23:19), and therefore, His reputation is on the line. However, you must get to know God in order to know exactly what that reputation is. If we become wise about God and His commitment to us, then it not only makes us wise about the directions in which He tells us to go, but it also gives us courage during those times when we have to rely more on our vision than we do our sight. That knowledge gives us boldness so that even in times when we can't see what the future holds, we're confident because we know who holds the future.

The fact of the matter is it's hard to trust what you don't know and understand. This is why it's so important for us to connect to God, so that we understand who's making a promise to us. The key here is that our fear is often eliminated with two things: knowledge and a solution. I submit to you that knowledge of God and the Spirit that He has provided *is* the solution. The more we learn to trust God in times of trepidation and uncertainty, the more we'll be able to eliminate the fear that often paralyzes us, even to the extent that we're afraid to go where God has told us to go.

2. Keep the known (God) above the unknown (the outcome)

If we come to know God and His unlimited power, it should be easier to trust Him in difficult times and situations. Most of the fear that we feel comes from not knowing how things will turn out. For example, there was Moses, hearing what God was commanding him to do, but being unsure of how it was all gonna work out. A man that had killed a man some 40 years prior, and God allowed him to live and didn't allow any harm to come to him, and yet, Moses could only see the obstacles and not the finish line.

Even when it isn't clear what the end is gonna look like, we must be clear on what God's provisions look like. If you know that God always provides, then how He does so shouldn't be of a greater concern to you. I know we like details, but we must also understand that God can't always trust us with the details. The Bible tells us that God hardened Pharaoh's heart after he sent Moses to lead the captives to freedom (Exodus 7:3-4). Imagine how Moses, who was already hesitant, felt when God told him that He was going to do that. Imagine what you would do if God told you of every struggle that came with the promise.

So our fears can be further eliminated by keeping what we know about God in the forefront of our minds. If we think about it, many of us have accomplished things that we never would've believed had we known what it was gonna require of us. Many of us have gone places in our lives that only God could've taken us. It's to our benefit to remember those things when we're more concerned with how it's gonna end up than we are with who's gonna get us there.

The saints of old would often say "If it had not been for The Lord on my side, where would I be?" They understood that God had kept them through the unseen and unknown, and they arrived at their destination as planned. Not without trouble, not without issues, and not without some personal uncertainty along the way. But it was God's keeping them in spite of it all that let them know that the next time they were facing an unknown future, the same God that delivered before would be able to do it again.

3. Excuses are a precursor to failure

"Whether you think you can or you can't, you're right." – Henry Ford

While this quote from Henry Ford isn't Scripture, there's wisdom is his words. There's nothing that we can do to limit God's power, but there is something that we can do to block our blessings and our successes. God is not short on His promises, as we've discussed, but our inability to step out on faith can limit our ability to receive the promise.

One of the saddest things about us is even when we know God, what He's done for us, and what we've seen Him do for others, we're not afraid to go back and forth with Him.

We're not afraid to tell Him what we can't do, all the while, forgetting who we're talking to. We fail to understand that God isn't giving us ideas, dreams, and plans for a better and more prosperous life without plans to bring it to fruition. How is it, then, that we come up with excuses before we even try to execute?

Before we make excuses about what God has called us to accomplish, we should consider these things:

- **When He calls you, you won't have all the tools** – We're often called before we're ready. Therefore, we're not able to prepare beforehand. When the call comes, that's the time for preparation, not excuses

- **You will often feel smaller than what you're called to accomplish** – God has often called minor people to major responsibilities. There's a difference between humility and fear, and God knows when you're trying to hide from the challenge

- **It won't always be easy, and that's by design** – God will challenge you to see if you trust Him. Don't let the fact that it isn't easy discourage you.

- **Remember, when you can't, God can!** – His strength is made perfect in your weakness. Remember that God has put himself on the line. If you follow His lead, you won't fail

Many of us are defeated before we start because we begin coming up with all of the reasons that we can't do something that God has put on us. However, the easiest way to fail is for you to defeat yourself. As many doubters and naysayers that we have in our lives, we must acknowledge the fact that they aren't always painting on a blank canvas. That means that in order for those people to be effective, we have to show up with some preloaded doubt of our own. We have to have already told ourselves that it might not work before they show up to confirm it.

As we've already discussed 2 Timothy 1:7, if God didn't give us a spirit of fear, then that spirit came from somewhere else, and anything that isn't of God is evil. Before you allow the devil to steal your dreams, I encourage you once again to tap into the Spirit that God gave you. Do that, and you're already victorious.

4. He didn't bring you this far to abandon you

Many of us will find ourselves knee deep in the promises of God, only to wonder if we should turn around and go back. Consider those Children of Israel that Moses was charged with leading to the Promised Land. At the first sign of discomfort, many were ready to go back into captivity. They were ready to go back to a place of bondage, rather than press forward to the promise of God. How many of you have that testimony?

What we must remember is that God is not just a beginning of the promise God, nor is He just an end of the promise God. He's also an along the way God. That means that even in those moments where you're questioning whether or not you went the right way, took the right risks, or even questioning whether or not you really heard God's voice telling you to do what you're doing, He's still right there. And though there are times when we may feel all alone, we must remember that He didn't bring us to the wilderness to abandon us. There is a greater purpose.

Sometimes we begin to question what we've done because we don't see the support that we think we should, we don't see people that we started out with, or we don't see the provisions for what it is that we're doing. I can tell you from experience that there can be no fear like chasing after something so big, something that God wakes you up in the middle of the night about, and you look around and there's seemingly no one there to catch you if you fall.

There is no fear like God telling you to do something that, in your mind, you know it takes a group of people to do, but you look around and the group you're in isn't prepared to do anything about your dream. That's fear. But God is even bigger than that!

I submit to you that God will feed you out of nowhere. I submit to you that God will bless you financially out of nowhere. I submit to you that God will send help, sometimes from unexpected sources, out of nowhere. As the saints of old still say, "He's a way out of no way", and if you examine that statement, you'll see just how great God is. He's an ever present help in times of trouble. I promise, He didn't bring you this far to abandon you.

Conclusion

As we stated in the open of this chapter, fear paralyzes us. It cause us to sit down when God has called us to action. Not only does it attack us, but it attacks those around us. It cause people to speak their fears and anxieties of what we're doing into our lives and then we become frozen. But if God gave you a vison, you can't let the devil take that away from you by causing you to tap into the wrong spirit.

Some of us are sitting on million dollar ideas all because of fear. Some of us have been living unhappily ever after for decades because we listened to someone else that didn't quite understand just how passionate we were or how hard we were willing to work. And yes, some of us have mortgaged our futures because we saw our own limitations more clearly that we saw the possibilities with God. We must overcome that fear.

It's been noted that the Children of Israel wandered 40 years before they made it to the Promised Land. Geographic studies show that the trip from the Red Sea to what God had promised them should've only taken just over a few weeks to reach. Disobedience, a lack of faith, and fear of the unknown kept them from what God promised. God still delivered, but

He delivered to a generation that was ready for what He promised.

Many of us are wandering aimlessly out of fear. We haven't addressed that burning desire that God has placed in our spirit. We haven't conquered that one thing that has held us back from our destiny. We've made so many excuses about why we can't do what God said we should and could do. And it's not all about material prosperity. Many relationships remain broken because we haven't confronted the things that God has told us to. Fear of rejection has kept us from some happy relationships that God has promised us.

My prayer is that we overcome the Pharaoh of fear that exists in our lives. If you really believe that God can, stop telling yourself that you can't. Remember that when God makes a promise, He commits Himself to it and He will swear by His own name because there is no name greater (Hebrews 6:13). Even when it seems as if you can't see the outcome, trust God more than you fear failure. You never know, you could be just a few weeks from your blessing.

Chapter 6

Pharaoh: Failure

Nobody likes to lose and nobody likes to fail at whatever it is they're trying. The theme of this book centers on Moses confronting Pharaoh. All of Moses' apprehension was centered on whether or not he could be successful. He saw his limitations, but not a limitless God. He saw all the ways in which Pharaoh would resist before he saw the ways in which God could make Pharaoh submit. He was afraid of failure. He wanted assurances that He would win.

Moses was just like we are. We'd try anything if we thought we'd win everything. If we never thought that we'd fail, God would be able to get us to move at His word. Sure, we claim to be listening for God's voice and we claim to be willing to do whatever God tells us to do, but the moment things don't go as *we* planned, we contemplate throwing in the towel.

Failure has the ability to make victors of a few and cowards of many. Many of us can't handle rejection or defeat, and yet, we expect to be victorious. We never expect our circumstances to have the upper hand on us, and when they do, we often look to bail out. But as the saying goes, anything worth having is worth working for, and that includes our freedom. For every slave under Pharaoh's rule, there's a different hindrance that he'll use to keep us bound.

Before I get to outlining some of the character building things that we must take from not always being successful, we must understand that there are some things about success that are not optional. These are things that I call life's "have to's". These are things that we struggle with, but we must conquer if we're going to be successful.

No matter what you're trying to be successful at in life (relationships, business, family, ministry, church), there are some things that aren't optional. Depending on what you're doing, you must determine those things that you can't and won't compromise on for the sake of your success and stick to it! If you don't have any "have to's" in your life, you don't have any discipline. If you don't have any discipline, then you're courting failure with a promise to marry it.

Many of us are struggling with the "have to's" in our lives. We sit around complaining, procrastinating, and putting on the back burner things that aren't optional. There are some things in your life that you HAVE TO do. For your survival, for your peace of mind, for your success, for your overall well-being, and for your life's fulfillment. You need these things done! You must put emphasis on your "have to's"!

When you treat a "have to" in your life like it's not important, like it's secondary, or like it doesn't matter, you'll look up and find that all the things that are prominent in your life are things that don't add any real value to your life. And if you're not careful, you'll find that the people around you aren't "have to" people as well. They're people that are optional as it pertains to whether or not you will succeed or fail.

So how do we navigate in our lives so that the inevitability of failure doesn't become something that kills our dreams completely? How do we maintain our focus when what we poured ourselves into falls flat, either momentarily or permanently? What can you learn when your dreams lay in pieces at your feet? Here are some things that I've learned as someone that has often gone against the traditional rules of what some would consider the paths to success:

1. There are no straight paths to success

The book you're reading right now is the 10th one I've written. To this point, I've never had a New York Times Best Seller (I pray that you're holding my first one right now!). I've never been on Oprah's Book Club. I'm a self-published author who felt inspired one day to exercise a gift that God gave me from an early age. My primary goal in writing was to help someone, but like many others with a gift, I want to be successful as well. I want spiritual compensation as well as monetary compensation, and in that order.

What I've found as I've journeyed on in these 11 years of being published and 30 plus years of writing is that there are many ups and downs when you're trying to build something from the ground up. Entrepreneurship isn't the same as getting a job in a company and working your way up. At your job, if you punch in and punch out, you get paid your wages or you quit. When you're in business for yourself, you punch in, punch out, punch back in, and punch back out, work all hours of the day and night and you may not make a dime some months. But because you have a burning desire, you can't just quit.

In order to truly be successful, particularly when you're working for yourself, you have to be willing to weather the storms. You have to be willing to navigate crooked and bumpy roads. You have to be able to walk in darkness, not ever really seeing where you're going at times. Yes, you have to have some unbelievable faith, not just in God, but also in yourself. If success was a straight and lighted path, we'd all be doing just fine. But there are some challenges along the way.

You'll also have to navigate the criticisms of well-meaning people that will advise you to give up because your success wasn't instant and overnight. You'll have to bob and weave when people are throwing jabs at you like "How long will this take" or "You should do that on the side", not realizing that they're devaluing your dreams with every word they say.

You'll have to avoid certain functions and certain people because you have no desire to be discouraged, as you're more aware than they are that you're on a long journey because in many cases, it's taking longer than YOU thought it would too. Let's be real, we sometimes beat ourselves up before anyone else gets the chance to with words like "Am I good enough", "Is this really gonna work" and "How long will it take before I can show them that my dream was valid".

Not only must these facts be understood by the person seeking to be successful, but it also must be understood by those around that person. People will try and convince you to stay captive by "playing it safe", when what will actually make you happy is living out your dreams. Some people just don't realize how uncomfortable a "safe" place is to a person that was called to do more.

For example, a person with a prison mentality will often fail to see the bars of the prison that has them caged. Eventually, they come to identify and accept the conditions of captivity. They come to say things like "Well, at least I have a place to lay my head and 3 meals a day". They lose sight of the fact that being captive in any situation isn't freedom. No matter how we adjust to the conditions, prison is still prison, and it's never an ideal situation. No matter how we come to appreciate him on some twisted level, Pharaoh is holding us captive and he's not our friend just because he's keeping us alive.

The mentality that success didn't come easy or overnight, and therefore you throw in the towel, is a mentality that suggests that we surrender to our conditions and be what our current situation says we should be. Something that I've always shared with people when they asked how it is that I took such a chance on me are these two things:

- **I have a supportive wife** – The fact that my wife not only believed in what God had called me to do, but she supported me, encouraged me, jumped in and worked with me, and was even disappointed in me when doubt would creep in and I would threaten to go get a "regular job", is something so invaluable that I can't even measure it. You don't always need everyone to support you. You just need the right someone to do that.

- **Trial and error is essential to success** – We purchase and use products every day that were designed and invented by people that tried and failed over and over and over again. We see the destination that they had in mind on our store shelves, online, and anywhere else we can purchase goods and services. But the only way that we'll ever see the long and winding road that it took to be successful is if they tell us their story. And believe me, if you're successful at anything, there's a story to be told.

It remains true that whatever we desire to do in life, whether it's business, marriage, relationships, raising a family, or whatever, there's going to be some trial and error. Even those that choose to play it safe on a 9 to 5 will have some struggles as they climb the corporate ladder. And let's be clear, some people are working a 9 to 5 at places they wanna be. They actually are living out their dreams. There's nothing wrong with the traditional job structure if that's where you wanna be, but that's not for everyone. But even in those situations, there are peaks and valleys. No one has sustained success without a challenge somewhere.

What we must be careful of is allowing others to determine the parameters of our success. For many, success is determined by finances and possessions. If you don't have a lot of either, then you're a failure to them. For others, success is security and comfort. The stability of a regular and consistent income, with something set up for retirement. But what must be remembered is what's success in one life is misery in another.

People with much in the way of finance and possessions are often miserable. People with a secure job and a waiting nest egg are often unfulfilled because they didn't go after what they *really* wanted in their lives. The parameters of your success should be determined by the person that gave you the vision.

If God's plan was for me to write just to influence the people around me to be better, then I'm successful. If His plan was for me to write as much as I can so that my children could live off my legacy, then I'm successful. If His plan was in fact for me to be rich and famous, but through attrition and hard work over decades of writing, then I shall be successful.

Whatever it is that you have ventured to be through the vision that God has given you for your life, it is He that will determine what your success looks like. To use myself again as an example, my books aren't a success when they're sold, they're a success when they're completed. True accomplishments aren't measured by what we've gained. They're measured by what we've achieved.

2. Character is formed in adversity

The adversity that we face during our trials and our failures is in fact what develops us. It's in the adversities of the long and winding road to success that we learn just how fragile our dreams can be. It's during those times that we develop not only what it takes to be successful, but also what it takes to stay that way. However success is defined for you, you'll need some grit and determination to maintain it. Nothing can teach you that like falling on your face can.

I understand that none of us like to fall short, but there are so many lessons that can be learned from our failed efforts. I often tell people to learn to see God in everything, and where you can't see God, you should *seek* God. Believe it or not, there are times when God made it hard for us, just as He did for Moses by the hardening of Pharaoh's heart. There are times when we claim a faith that hasn't been tested, so God puts us through it by allowing a few no's to come our way and allowing a few doors to be slammed in our faces.

The question must be asked of us as we pursue our life's dreams: How bad do you want it? That question must be answered in what we're willing to go through to get to where we say we wanna be. If you're ready to give up at the first sign of trouble (we'll discuss that in the next section), then you should be wondering whether or not what you're pursuing is for you. It's not enough to just be talented or gifted in something. You have to be courageous enough, tough enough, and mentally strong enough to endure. Whenever you're chasing your calling, your purpose, your passion, or your career, know that it will be a marathon and not a sprint.

Excitement will only take you so far. Enthusiasm will only take you so far. Just wanting it so bad will only take you so far. Even drive has its limitations. It's what you do with opportunities that matter, and even more so, it's what you do when there are no opportunities or when opportunity is snatched away from you by forces that are working against you.

It's not just about God's promises to you, but it's also about whether or not you'll let God mold you into the person that you need to be in order to live out the promise He's made to you. If you read your Bible carefully, God often promised prosperity to the unprepared, the uncertain, the unwilling, and often the unqualified. It wasn't until He molded them to fit the promise that He'd made to them that they were able to live out their purpose.

The benefit of your adversity is in the fact that it often prepares you for the next challenge. Even if the next challenge is unique in nature and something that you've never seen before, if nothing else, you come to rely on the fact that God brought you out before, and He can do it again. It's during those times when things aren't working out that we learn to see God working it out.

During those moments when it seems that nothing will ever go right, that's the time when we must draw on the strength that God has been developing in us through our various trials, disappointments, and failures. James 1:3 tells us that the trying of our faith brings patience in us. Even if God isn't the cause of your adversity, it is God that can make you stronger through your adversity. It is God that can help us to overcome when we feel overwhelmed.

3. Failure will often weed out the frauds

Like it or not, many of us can testify to having some fraudulent dreams and aspirations at some points in our lives. It's often when things don't go as we planned that we find out whether or not what we thought we wanted was really valid. Some things look good on paper and in our heads, but when the reality of the work is staring us in the face, we sometimes shrink under the pressure.

Failure is something that will always tell us the truth about what we're doing, who we are, and whether or not we can endure. Something we've watched someone else do from a distance can seem so simple, but once we get into it for ourselves, we see how much it takes to do what they're doing. We see the late nights, the struggles, the headaches, and so on, and then we wonder how it's all being done. What some people have learned to do with ease can often send us running for the hills.

This is even more evident when it comes time to get people to support your dreams. You're trying to overcome all that it takes to live out your dreams and you sometimes need some human help along the way. People will pledge their undying support to you and they'll stand by your side, until the first sign of trouble comes. When it gets challenging, you find out that not everyone is up to the challenge. You find out that lip service isn't service at all.

Failure will expose the inadequacies and inefficiencies in us, in those around us, and in our plans to pursue our dreams. It tells us whether or not what we're doing is authentic, even before anyone else that doesn't understand the vision can. Not only will it teach you what you need to know about going forward, but it will also teach you about whether or not you're brave enough to do it.

Don't misunderstand the benefit of this, however. Being exposed as a fraud can help you to find your authentic self. It can help to either refocus you on what it is that you need to do in order to be successful, or it can help you to abandon something before you waste years, and even decades, pursuing something that isn't actually what you're called to do.

Lofty dreams and goals aren't real until you understand what it will take to get where you're going. What's your plan when the money isn't there? What's your plan when the support isn't there? What's the next move when you put your heart and soul into something, only to find out that your best isn't good enough, even on the ground floor of what you're trying?

How will you come back when you realize that you may have to do it all by yourself, or with the help of strangers because close family and friends won't sow into what you're doing? Whether or not you quit is what will determine whether or not you're a fraud or for real. Somewhere along the way, we're gonna be exposed to failure. We can either grow from it or wallow in it.

4. The only people that don't fail are the people that don't try (and that's failure too)

This is for those of us that are sometimes challenged about what we're doing from people that aren't doing anything. With all of this talk about trial and error, and trying and failing, the only thing that would be worse than that would be doing absolutely nothing at all. It's those in the peanut gallery that will tell you what you should and shouldn't be doing from the comfort of their seats. It's those people that will tell you to stop because they couldn't imagine doing what you're doing, not realizing that they aren't built like you.

Listening to people that have renamed their failure as success, when it's really just comfort, complacency, and contentment, is much too harsh for your delicate ears. Yes, we're sensitive about our goals and dreams, and while some negativity can be motivation to prove people wrong, too much negativity can discourage us to the point of sitting down on our gifts.

If there's ever anything that we do to make the Pharaoh of failure's job easy, it's not going after anything. It's not chasing, not pursuing, not being ambitious, and not being motivated about the call or the purpose. The only thing worse than being trapped by failed effort has to be being a willing slave to failure by just giving up altogether.

Make no mistake about it, many of our dreams are aborted because someone else thought that it was too hard for us, based on *their* limitations. It's similar to what we do to God when we call a situation impossible because we can't figure out how it can be done. We surrender to the devil when we sit down on what God has given us to do just because it may be a little bit challenging at times. Being in bondage is one thing, but being complicit in your bondage is something entirely different.

I understand that failure can knock the wind out of you. It can discourage you, it can cause you to doubt yourself, and even cause you to doubt the voice of God, who will often call us into dry places and tell us that something is gonna grow there eventually. But we all get knocked down, and contrary to popular belief, it's not just about whether or not you get up.

Many people have gotten up before in a fight when they probably should've stayed down. It's not just about getting up, but it's about getting up with wisdom. Are you gonna get up and fight? Are you gonna get up and try a better strategy? Or, are you gonna get up and walk away when you realize that you're fighting the wrong battle? Whatever you choose to do, the one thing you shouldn't choose is quitting when God is in the fight with you.

Conclusion

One of the things that causes us to struggle with failure is how big our dreams often are. We have a lot of grand ideas about how we want our lives to go, and when things don't go as planned, it can sometimes be devastating. However, I want to stress that a dream that doesn't challenge you may not be big enough. We ought to want some things in life that cause us to stretch beyond our limits. There ought to be some things that we chase in life that are beyond our immediate reach, but that will make us happy.

I also understand that life doesn't have to be all risk. There ought to be some basic things that we desire for ourselves that don't require us putting it all on the line. But there are times when even low hanging fruit will give us trouble. There are times when it seems as if the simple things in life have come to be complicated. Even when what we wanted wasn't too elaborate, we can still find ourselves falling short. So, how can we combat this?

Let me just state that I don't believe that failure itself is the issue as much as how failure makes us feel. Consider what it was like learning to ride a bike. You took the training wheels off and you gave it a shot. You were determined to make it work. Everyone else was riding a two-wheeler and you were gonna do it too. No doubt, you fell a few times while learning. That wasn't the only issue, though. Another issue was whether or not anyone saw you fall. It was the embarrassment of falling down in front of people. It was the people that laughed at you as you struggled to learn and achieve.

It's not so much the failing and trying again that gets us, because as I just illustrated, we're willing to try, try again for what we really wanna do. The question is, are there any people around to help me up? Are there any people that will train me so that the next time I get up on this bike, I might be successful? Are people more willing to point and laugh than they are to assist? Has anyone checked to see if I've hurt myself? Is there anyone willing to encourage me through my failure, so that I might feel secure in trying again?

Failure is a part of life and none of us are immune, but that feeling of being defeated, embarrassed, mocked for trying, and alone in defeat is something that we're not all built for. It's that kind of thing that will cause us to withdraw from people, withdraw from God, and go inward, never to live out our purpose in life. That feeling that's associated with failure is what can cause depression and anxiety, and it can cause apprehension and self-esteem issues. Failure is bound to come. Do you have people around you that will help you up?

Overcoming this is a group effort. When God sent Moses to confront Pharaoh, it wasn't just Moses alone. It was a group effort. Aaron had to play his part, and God surely played His part. In those moments when Pharaoh would not bend, God didn't allow Moses to sink into what seemed like failure because it didn't work the first time Moses said let the people go. In fact, what we can also learn from Moses is that success isn't automatic because we say "God said..". Putting God's name on it isn't always a motivator for people.

If you wanna be freed from the grips of the depression that failure can cause, keep some people around you that will motivate you. Keep some people around you that will encourage you to try again. Keep some people around you that will help you back up on the bike. Most importantly, keep some people around you that will tell you when it's not your fight to win. Not with an eye towards you giving up fighting, but with an eye towards you finding the fight you're supposed to be in. Keep some people around you that will help you to win, particularly when it seems as if all is lost.

Chapter 7

Pharaoh: Broken Relationships

At one point or another, all of us have had to deal with separation in a relationship. Not just the romantic type, mind you. Falling out with friends and family can often be more traumatic than breaking up with someone. We're sometimes under the false impression that friends and family aren't ever supposed to leave or forsake us. We believe that these long standing relationships have a never ending shelf life or an unbreakable bond. We believe that, until reality hits us square in the heart.

As I've grown in life and in ministry, I've seen just how devastating broken relationships can be and the damage they can do to all involved. Just like many of you reading this book, I've seen this type of thing in my own family. The hidden animosity, the unspoken grudges, the jealousy, the secret backstabbing, and so on. We all have that type of thing in our families, and even in our DNA, as we're all capable of such things, even if we don't practice them.

The truth of the matter is when we see such things and ignore them, we're actually ignoring cracks in the foundation. We're actually ignoring the very things that lead to a full blown break in our relationships. We don't confront anything, and we internalize everything. We harbor ill feelings and resent people until, quite honestly, all hell breaks loose. We do this with a mind towards preserving the relationship, when in fact, we're doing more harm than good.

When we fail to repair those little cracks and fractures along the way, we soon find out that the break is much more difficult to navigate. Sometimes, all it takes is one blowup to find out just how far from good you really are with a person. From one disagreement, we can find that a person has been holding in so much. What we thought was a minor leak turns in a dam bursting open.

I've often stated in my relationship writings that trust is a more important component to a relationship than love. Love always matters, but if you love someone that you can't trust, love begins to feel like a hindrance. It gnaws away at you because you love a person, but the fact that you can't trust them causes that love to be painful. When a relationship falls apart due to pinned up frustration and resentment, you have the issues before you, and you have the broken trust because you believed that you were in a relationship with someone that would've told you of such things before it went too far.

We must remember what true repentance requires of us. For example, contrary to popular belief, just telling God sorry isn't enough and doesn't represent true repentance. True repentance requires work. It requires effort. It requires us turning away from what caused us to be separated from God, and turning to what would put us back in His good graces. That effort of repentance is also required in our relationships with one another. It's not just about giving a token "I'm sorry". It's about the work of repairing what's broken.

This presents a series of hurdles that we must overcome if we're to be restored. A broken relationship can hold people, families, communities, and even nations captive for long periods of time because people aren't always willing to do what it takes to be restored. We often say things like "I'm not jumping through all of those hoops…", without realizing that we all must jump through or jump over something in order for things to in fact be restored.

Here is a truth that we all know, but sometimes won't acknowledge: There's a difference between a falling away in a relationships and a betrayal. Some relationships aren't broken, they just ended. However, the most difficult ones are the ones that have been broken through betrayal, mistrust, misuse, and simply a lack of care. Something that falls away is akin to clothes that you outgrow or that have become out of fashion. You just don't wear them anymore. A broken relationship is like a rip in a favorite pair of jeans that you're not quite done with just yet. You want them restored.

There are some hurdles that we need to look at in relation to the restoration of relationships. Let's look at these four hurdles and examine what's keeping us from not only being free from broken relationships, but also healed from them:

1. The Blame Hurdle

Let's be honest, usually the first thing we wanna do when a relationship falls apart is assess blame. And if we're really being honest, we often want to do that so that we'll know who to point at when someone asks "What happened?" It'd be nice if we were asking that question in the name of self-evaluation, but we know that's not the case. We wanna know who was at fault.

While it is important to know who was at fault, it is our reasoning for wanting this information that can cause us to lose sight of what's important. It's important to know who's at fault because this determines who's responsible in the way of forgiveness, both seeking and giving. We shouldn't beat ourselves up for things that aren't our fault, but we also shouldn't look to shift blame when we're responsible.

We often fail to properly identify fault because we get caught up on intent. One of our favorite excuses is "I didn't mean to". We must understand that unintentional harm is still harm and we must learn to apologize for our actions without excuses. This is the same mentality that causes us to pray to God by saying things like "Lord, *if* I've done anything wrong...", as if there were a possibility that we haven't. While I understand that we can sometimes do things without knowing what we've done, once it's made known to us, the "if" should go away.

To take this a step further, we don't get to determine the level of another's offense. If they're offended, we should apologize. Even if we're firm on our position, our intent should never be to hurt anyone with our stance. You can apologize for offense without changing your position.

I know it seems that we're off track here, but follow what I'm saying. Properly assessing blame begins with a willingness to properly self-evaluate. If nothing is ever your fault, then I'm confident that a lot of things actually are your fault, and you just won't acknowledge it. We can't properly jump the blame hurdle if all options aren't on the table:

- Is it actually your fault?
- Did someone hurt you unprovoked, or was it retaliation?
- Is there a misinterpretation, miscommunication, or misunderstanding somewhere?
- Even if what happened to you seems out of the blue, are you reaping something here that you've sown elsewhere?

That last one will trip a lot of us up. Some people have done things to us in life and God didn't stop it because we had it coming. Not that God endorses evil, but He will allow us to reap the harvest of what we may have sown in another's life. Sometimes, the only way we learn to treat people better is in first-hand experience on how we've treated others. Sometimes it's gotta come back to us before we learn. And even when we wanna blame somebody else, sometimes the only person to blame is us.

There are also times when we expose ourselves to some people that mean us no good. God will actually show us some signs that we're in the wrong place, and yet, we stay. I know it would seem easy to blame the person that hurts us, but at what point do we accept responsibility for staying in harm's way? We can't blame people for swinging and not blame ourselves for not ducking.

2. The Pride Hurdle –

Proverbs 16:18 (NLT) tells us that pride goes before destruction and haughtiness before a fall. The destruction of many a relationship and the delay in the repair (we'll discuss that in a moment) rests here. So many of us are so caught up in our pride and our positions that we fail to see what's really at stake. Pride can cause us to lose something valuable by trying to hold on to something trivial.

So many arguments that we have can be settled by us laying down our pride for what's right, as opposed to just wanting to be right. Let me explain that further. We could be two hundred percent right in our particular stance, and yet, we'll fail to stop somewhere and ask ourselves "Is being right at this moment worth the relationship?" We can see a relationship going off the rails, and yet we won't stop talking because we want to make our point. There must come a point where we decide that being understood doesn't always have to come at the expense of peace.

I can tell you from personal experience that I have hindered and damaged some relationships in my past because I was right and I could prove it. There were times in my life when my pride kept me from seeing that even though I was right, my insistence on making it known was damaging someone else. Some people know that they're wrong and are often embarrassed about it. Our insistence on reminding them of how wrong they are can cause them to go away from us.

What we often miss through the eyes of pride is the fact that there's often a shift in the relationship before it completely falls apart. What I mean is there's a shift from being comfortable to uncomfortable. A shift from being friendly to simply being cordial. There are times when a discussion gets so heated that even after everything is settled and things clam down a bit, the relationship may never be the same again. Its pride that will cause us to drive a point home, while at the same time, driving a wedge. You may have won the battle, and you may have even won the war, but we all know that what's often forgotten in combat are the casualties along the way.

The key to getting over the pride hurdle is in that Proverbs 16:18 text. There's a warning about what's coming. Destruction is coming. A fall is coming. In order to maintain what we have, we must do maintenance on our own pride. Pride is what keeps us pushing an issue when it may be best to let it die. Pride is what keeps us from letting some things go when we want to argue some more about it.

Laying down your pride isn't the same as allowing people to walk all over you. It doesn't make you weak, nor does it make you a pushover. In fact, it shows a great amount of strength to pause and reflect before you just react. Laying down your pride simply means that you value the relationship. It means that if tabling a conversation until it can be had from a safe, calm place is what's best, then that's what you're willing to do. It means that you value a constructive conversation over a shouting match any day of the week.

It isn't the disagreement that breaks the relationship, it's often the pride that does that. The unwillingness to admit wrong. The unwillingness to hold our peace instead of holding our position. The struggle to not let our anger rule the day and hold us hostage. The struggle to forgive when pride wants us to hold the grudge just a little bit longer. Relationships can handle a disagreement. What they often can't escape is the destruction caused by pride.

3. The Forgiveness Hurdle

It's amazing that the thing that often holds us hostage is our own inability to let it go. We can't be released because we won't release. The Pharaoh of forgiveness is one that holds so many of us bound at various points in our lives. But in order to get over this hurdle, we must be willing to get over ourselves. If we really wanna be free, we've got to surrender ourselves to forgiveness. The fact of the matter is there is indeed power in being free and setting some things in our lives free. You're not strong when you hold a grudge, because bearing the grudge is actually making you weak. No, you are your strongest when you learn how to let go.

We often withhold forgiveness because we think that gives us control. In fact, we do our best to assume the position of Pharaoh, wielding our so-called power, holding the captives under our thumb while we decide if they're worthy to be free. What we fail to realize is withholding forgiveness is its own prison. Just like Pharaoh, who couldn't see the energy he was expending in his futile attempt just to keep the Children of Israel under his thumb, we often don't realize just what it takes to stay mad all the time.

The pride that we just spoke about in the last section creeps in and tells us that if repentance doesn't come in the exact way that we feel that it should, we will resist it in any form. We fool ourselves into believing that we can see the heart just as God does, often trying to measure the sincerity of an apology, as opposed to recognizing that all intentions are to be judged by The Almighty.

Getting past the anger that causes us not to forgive means not getting caught up in what we feel we deserve. An apology from someone that's wronged us is the right thing to do, but we've got to learn to be okay if it never comes. We've got to accept the fact that everyone doesn't have the same moral compass that we do. We've got to understand that some people will stand their ground, even to the point of losing fellowship with us. What we must protect against is becoming that same type of person.

It's much too easy to get caught up in another's unforgiving spirit, so much so, that we fail to see that if not for the grace of God, we'd be the same way. We'd find ourselves developing a grudge when there once wasn't one, all because of what we feel we deserve. Forgiveness is a slippery slope on both sides. If we don't plan to approach it in a godly way, we make reconciliation that much more difficult.

4. The Restoration Hurdle

If we wanna be free from the pain and disappointment that comes with a broken relationship, restoration must always be the ultimate goal. If we don't always have an eye towards restoration, a broken relationship can leave us trapped in the past. When we consider our relationship with God, there was always an eye towards restoration with man, even before we fell. Why don't we have that same mentality with one another?

As forgiveness is the act of letting it go, restoration is the work of letting it go. It's not about making things "perfect", but rather it's the work of getting the relationship back to a place where it's functional and useful. The struggle that we often have with broken relationships is in how we can put them back together. The struggle is in the fact that things might never be the same again, but that doesn't mean that restoration isn't possible. It takes some work. It takes some healing. It takes some moments of discomfort. It takes a willingness to release what's holding you back. But restoration has to be the goal.

The fact that things may never be the same again can cause us to feel trapped, as if there's nothing else that we can do. When that's the case, many of us will refuse to try and salvage what we can. If we can't have what we once had, then we pout and act as if we don't want anything at all. But in order to be restored, we can't do things the same way we did them before. If we're paying attention, what we did before is what led us to being broken.

Being in right relationship with God requires some adjustments and some changes along the way. We were once enemies of Him, and yet, Christ died for the ungodly. If things go back to being the same, then we go back to our broken state. The same is true when we want to repair our broken relationships with one another. We must examine what caused us to become broken, and vow to never be that way again. Things may not be the same again, and that's actually a good thing.

Restoration requires contrition out of us. It requires us to go further than the words "I apologize". It requires a desire to be healed, even if we aren't made completely whole again. If we want to get to a place where our relationships are restored, we can't go into restoration with the same mentality and the same attitude that got us broken in the first place. It's not just about us changing how we deal with one another, but it's also about changing how we receive one another. It's about accepting the fact that disagreements don't have to turn into disintegration. We can always rebuild!

Conclusion

If we don't get anything else out of this chapter, we must get this: Two of the most important elements to maintaining a relationship are apologies and accountability. If people can just learn to apologize when they're made aware that someone feels wronged, as opposed to when they *feel* as if they've wronged someone, we'd be better off. That's an apology and accountability in a nutshell. When you've done wrong, accept responsibility and apologize. Otherwise, Pharaoh holds you hostage!

What becomes broken will often become weakened first. As we look to be freed from the bondage of a relationship that fell apart, we mustn't be confused about what led us to be broken in the first place. All of the things that lead to a breakdown must be examined, lest we wind up repeating the same mistakes that caused division. And as we examine, we must do so honestly. Lies lead to repetition of the same bad habits. Be honest with yourself and be honest with others. That's the only way to truly mend what's broken.

However, there is another side to this broken relationships thing. Whether we want to admit it or not, there is a time when we must say goodbye to some people. Their time is up. Their season is up. We may find out through disagreement or discomfort, but the truth of the matter is sometimes God orders a break-up. He exposes some things in a whisper, but when we ignore Him, things get loud and uncomfortable. We mustn't be afraid to disconnect from some people when the relationship is no longer good for all involved.

It doesn't mean that we wish them any ill will, nor does it mean that we harbor any bad feelings, but if we're not careful, we can find ourselves trapped by unnecessary obligation. We can find ourselves committed to something that's failing because it wasn't meant to last forever.

Everyone that started with us weren't necessarily meant to finish with us. And we have to be okay with that.

The reality is nothing lasts forever and all relationships aren't separated by death only. But for those that God meant to be together, we should do our part to hold them together. When they come apart, we should do our best to make room for Him to repair them. If they've reached an end, we should allow Him to heal us after the separation so that we aren't forever trapped by resentment and scenarios of "what if".

Remember, it's not always about being whole again. Sometimes it's just about being healed. You may not be the same again, but that doesn't mean that you're not alright. Healing is a process and pain is a prison. The grudge and the guilt is a weight to bear, but I've never seen anyone crushed under the weight of forgiving someone. We have to decide how bad we wanna be free and what we're willing to pay. It's all in how we choose to look at our battle scars. They're not only a representation of what's happened to us, but they're also a representation of what we've survived.

Chapter 8

Pharaoh: Abandonment and Low self-esteem

Whether we understand it or not, our self-esteem is directly connected to the people that we currently have in our lives, and also the people from our past. High self-esteem is often a direct result of positive reinforcement, while low self-esteem can be the result of the opposite. High self-esteem can also come from unhealthy praise, as some people are made to feel as if they're better than others. At the same time, low self-esteem can come from forms of mental, physical, and sexual abuse, where people are made to feel as if they have no value.

This sets the atmosphere for a range of emotions as it relates to low self-esteem and abandonment issues. When the people that we feel ought to be there for us in a certain capacity aren't there, it can cause us to question our own worth. And when we don't have a strong sense of self-worth, we can feel less-than when people walk away from us, even when the people that are walking away aren't that significant in our lives. It's understood that we all need to learn how to deal with rejection, but when rejection has been your way of life, you either become numb to the pain, or overly sensitive to it. Both mentalities are unhealthy.

We're all products of our environments, which can at times be frustrating because we had no choice in where we were placed. There are some negative things that have been written on us from the time we were born that can, and often do, carry on into our adult lives. It effects our actions, our decision making, and our destiny if we aren't careful. I don't claim to have any clinical diagnosis, but I can offer spiritual observations.

For those of us that come from places that are deemed less-than by the masses, we understand that people will often try and put us down because of that fact. I'm reminded of what they said about Jesus in John 1:46 (NKJV): "Can anything good come out of Nazareth?" It's that kind of thinking that will cause people to try and put you down without even knowing what God has sent you here to be and do.

The Bible tells us that all that we've been through, Jesus Himself felt when He was on earth (Hebrews 4:15). There's no doubt that He felt a sense of abandonment as He went to the cross, looking down to see only one disciple present. So it would seem that some abandonment is a result of people not being able to help you endure the cross that you have to bear in your life.

This can cause us to feel isolated and alone, which in some cases, is God's plan. While abuse and people rejecting you because of where you're from isn't a godly thing to do, when we're called to do great work in the Kingdom, isolation is a part of the assignment. Abandonment comes with the territory. Not knowing whether or not you can make it is just what happens.

But what do we do when the abandonment that we feel isn't necessarily ministry related? What do we do when it seems as if we're being rejected by friends and family, when all we're trying to do is good? How do we keep our self-esteem high when it seems as if all people want to do is bring us down? On this Christian journey, how do we keep from feeling so alone and helpless when people turn their backs on us, and how do we keep it from destroying our confidence?

My issues have issues

When people have issues with love, being hurt, or emotional and physical abuse in their past, any type of rejection feels like abandonment. Even if the reasons for the rejection are valid, it can send them into a spiral that they feel they can't recover from.

What this does is hinder all the relationships that they have. Any slight is magnified. Any disagreements are catastrophic. Any admonishing, even if it's necessary, feels like an attack. People then begin walking on eggshells around them or just walking away from them altogether. So, how can we help people that feel rejected and abandoned because past issues keep showing up in their current day behavior? What do we do about people that feel like they're weighing everybody down with their constant need to be lifted up?

One of the things that we must realize is that damaged people are often wearing masks. Many of the people that we're seeing on a day to day basis, or each Sunday in church, are dealing with some issues that are hidden, but quite complex. At any given time, you could be talking to someone that's been sexually assaulted, molested, or physically abused. This type of thing is happening in homes, schools, churches, doctor's offices, and many other places where one is believed to be safe. And it's not just children. This type of behavior happens in marriages, between co-workers, with neighbors, and yes, even in families.

If you're aware of this, then you come to understand how low self-esteem rears its head in some people's lives. You come to understand why some people feel abandoned and left alone when certain relationships don't work out. Even if it's ultimately for the best, it just feels like one more person letting you down, using you, or throwing you away.

Many of these demons are often hidden, and unless you're trained to spot certain things, you'll have no idea why people lash out in their behavior. Unless you have some sort of experience in dealing with these things, you won't understand that some people aren't being difficult, complicated, or troublesome just for the sake of being that way, but their behavior is often a defense mechanism used to mask some deeper pain that they're feeling. Once you know all of these things, you won't be dismissive about their issues with a simple "Get over it", "You need The Lord" or "It ain't that serious".

What I must be clear about is my belief that professional outside counselling is key. I know sometimes in the church we don't often like to use people on the outside, but I believe that's a mistake. While our pastors and leaders can provide great spiritual counsel in many different areas, and God is ultimately the answer to whatever we're facing, I believe that sometimes it's best to seek counsel outside the church walls. Not just any type of counsel, but godly counsel.

I believe that God has provided us with some God-fearing counselors that can not only help people in a clinical sense, but they can also provide some Biblical and spiritual support to the counsel that the church gives. Some of these issues that we see in people are much more complex than "Just go pray about it". Prayer is the key, but facing the demons of the past that haunt us in the present must also be addressed.

Here are a few things that we must do when we're coming to grips with the issues that affect our self-esteem:

- **Name your affliction** – Again, I'm a firm advocate of Luke 18:1 ("Men ought always to pray") and 1 Thessalonians 5:17 ("Pray without ceasing"). However, we can't tell a person that's been molested or assaulted to pray it away without acknowledging that it happened and that it has an effect on who they are today. Whatever the issue is that's affecting your self-esteem, God knows all about it, but that doesn't mean that we don't have to learn to name it. Not so that God knows, but so that we're clear on what we're battling

- **If you're responsible, own that** – This can be difficult to determine as some of the things that affect us now are the results of things that happened when we were powerless to stop it. But even as we know what may be the cause of certain behavior, at some point we become aware, and thus we must become accountable. When you're able to see yourself in the mirror, you can't try and change the reflection without changing the person. We must identify when we go from victim to participant.

- **Healing is available** – We don't have to continue being what we were. While God won't erase your past, He can deliver you from it. He can reset some things in your life and cause you to rise above what once was, so that you can be what He's called you to be. Can anything good come out of your brokenness? With God, nothing shall be impossible!

When our issues aren't addressed, they permeate every area of life. They affect relationships, both romantic and platonic. They affect jobs, careers, friendships, and even family relationships. When we fail to deal with some of our self-esteem and abandonment issues, we simply feed the issue until it overtakes us.

With that being said, we must realize that everything that happens to us isn't necessarily abandonment or an attack on our self-esteem. There are some things that happen in our lives that are God-ordered. While it may seem as if we're under attack, we may simply be in transition. So rather than feel abandoned, we may just need to adjust.

Here are four things that you need to know that call more for understanding than they do someone to blame:

1. Seasons Change

We've all heard the statement that some people are only in our lives for a season, and that's true. I've even stated in some of my writings that some people are just a part of the landscape of our lives, passing by for the sake of scenery. Once you've gone past them, you may or may not ever pass that way again. With this changing of the seasons that often comes in our lives, we'd be best served if we didn't get attached to certain people.

If you live in a place like Michigan where I live, you get used to changing weather. The running joke is that if you don't like the weather in Michigan, wait 5 minutes and it'll change. At any time in the summer, a thunder storm could pop up. In the late fall or spring, we've seen inches of snow and 65 degree weather in the same week, one making it look as if the other never happened. And the reality is some of our relationships are just as volatile and unpredictable as Michigan weather. Some people are here today and gone tomorrow.

As the seasons change in our lives just like weather, the landscape also changes. With the change of weather, different things become necessary. Wardrobe changes are made. How we drive needs to be adjusted. What we can and can't do outdoors changes. So it goes when the seasons change in our lives. Some people that were okay for a certain season become less necessary for the next. Some people that can't handle certain weather will move to a warmer or cooler climate, as is their want.

Unfortunately, we don't know what we have in friends, associates, or otherwise until there's a change in season that occurs in our life (we'll talk more on that in a few paragraphs). There are some people that will only be around when it's sunny and 75 to 80 in your life. There are some people that only wanna be around when the water is warm and there's plenty of good times to be had on the beach of your life. However, when that shift comes, and the water gets rough, and the temperature drops, so will their attendance in your life.

So, we must ask ourselves, is this all bad? I know there's some disappointment when there's a shift in the weather of our lives and our so-called friends, and sometimes significant others, will scatter and thin out. But if it weeds some people out of our lives, aren't we the better for it? Again, understand that some people are assigned to our lives only for a season. There's a lesson to be learned, some growth that needs to take place, and then they're gone. It may be uncomfortable to think about, but sometimes that's what happens.

I know we like to say things like "This is my season" when things are going well or we're expecting them to turn around, but the reality is, whatever season we're in is our season. Whatever you're going through is your season, and unfortunately, some people can't handle you when you're down. The only way you're going to be able to find that out is when you're actually down. Depending on who's walking away, this can be disheartening, but know that when seasons do change, they tend to change again.

2. People Change

As we just discussed, we will sometimes make the assumption that people changed on us, when in reality, the weather in your life changed and their true colors were simply revealed. However, there are times in our lives when people will actually change on us. There are times when people will quite honestly become brand new on you. At times, they'll walk out of your life like you never knew one another.

This is where we must look for that silver lining in people exiting our lives. I'm of the belief that if people have two faces, you don't need them in your life. We're all better off when things are consistent. Even if a person is consistently against you, it's good to at least know that, and you're better off when you understand that.

We must be clear here, however. Everybody that changes on you isn't necessarily doing so because they're fake or disloyal. We sometimes forget that just as we evolve and grow, so do other people. They sometimes grow away from us for their own personal purposes, and we've got to be okay with that.

As we discussed in the previous section, people are sometimes just a part of the scenery of your life. Well, we can't be so self-centered that we don't understand that we're sometimes a part of somebody else's scenery. We're passing through someone else's life. Yes, we too can be seasonal. So even as people may change on you, before you get angry, before you get depressed, before you start casting blame, do a little evaluation. Maybe this change is what was needed. Maybe it was for the best.

3. Circumstances change

The circumstances which caused some people to be in our lives may in fact change and cause people to take flight. Not always because they're opportunists, but let's be clear, many times that is the case. Some people won't even answer a call for help from you unless they can see how you being whole benefits them. Those that love you benefit from your happiness because if you're happy, they're happy. However, those that are opportunists will only be around when it suits them.

It's unfortunate that we're involved with people that only want to be near us when it benefits and suits them, but such is life. The less you can do for some people, the less they want anything to do with you. This is why it's critical to take inventory of those that are with you when you have not, as opposed to those that are with you when you have.

When your resources thin out, people will thin out. Sometimes because you can't help them, and other times because they either can't or won't help you. Yes, some people will disappear on you when you fall just so that they don't have to help you up. You may have been there for them, but they have no intentions on being there for you. I know it hurts, but you're going to have to forgive and move on. For your own peace of mind, you have to accept that people won't always have the same heart as you.

Some of the abandonment issues that we face in life sometimes isn't personal. People were literally around you because things were good with you. Everybody likes a good time, and some people were near you because times were good. This can definitely effect our self-esteem because we all wanna be liked for who we are, not what we have. We all wanna be loved for the person we are, not for nefarious reasons.

When the circumstances change in our lives, it could mean any number of things. Our finances could be low when they were once high. We could experience health challenges, job loss or job promotion, marriage or separation/divorce. Who you're connected to during any of these times can often determine whether or not you'll go through these changes with support or with no one at all.

4. God never changes

In our need for consistency from people that are often inconsistent, there's comfort in the fact that God never changes. There's comfort in the fact that even as seasons change, people change, and circumstances change, we serve an unchanging God. We serve a God that's stable in who He is and what He does. He neither sleeps nor slumbers and His love isn't based on who we are, what we have, or what we can do for Him. It's based in who He is as God. He loves us regardless.

I understand that it's often hard to look past all of the pain and rejection that we feel and see in the physical in our day to day lives, but faith isn't something that we just acquire. It's something that we must practice. We must work each and every day to trust God more than we fret over who was or wasn't there for us in our time of need.

In our search for consistent love, companionship, and support, we must first put our faith and trust in The One that can consistently give love, without delay, without hesitation, and without ulterior motives. Not only can God provide us with that level of consistency in His being, He can also guide us to people that can provide the measure of love that we're looking for in our human existence.

Whether we admit it or not, we all feel the need to be validated. We want to know that we're loved, valued, and appreciated. This is why I don't understand why we've begun to preach less about sin and more about God's benevolence. His love for us is shown in His hatred of sin. Not that God hates us, but He hates our conduct when it's outside of His Word.

God shows His love by correcting us when we behave in ways that would cause us to be separate from Him. That should be preached, taught, and reinforced every chance we get. We should stress that God loves us so much, that He'll correct us, so that we may one day be with Him. He loves us so much that He sent His Son to die on the cross so that we have a way of being reconciled to Him. Rather than abandon us, He made a way for us to always be together.

Conclusion

Ultimately, the way out is through forgiveness. Whether your feelings of abandonment and low self-esteem are based in what happened to you or just how you feel, there must be a moment of forgiveness. You can't overcome anything that you refuse to let go of. I'm not saying it will be easy, because depending on what happened to us, forgiveness can take a great deal of strength. But finding the strength to forgive is much easier than finding the strength each and every day to carry past burdens, issues, and pain around with you.

There are things that happened to us, but they didn't happen because of us. We must forgive ourselves for being present, but not at fault. What that means is that we sometimes blame ourselves for things that happened to us because we didn't stop it. Sometimes, we could have. Other times, we were powerless. Either way, what's past is past and you must protect your current and future self by forgiving. So how do we go about getting that done? Maybe it's through counseling or confronting (in a peaceful way) the person that damaged you, but you've got to be willing to let it go.

This particular Pharaoh is often one of the most difficult to defeat because you actually have to face your oppressor about *your own* freedom, and not the freedom of something or someone else that's being held against their will. When you've been moved from foster home to foster home, and abandonment becomes the norm, you feel as powerless as

Moses did when God told him to go up against an Egyptian empire, armed only with a mandate from God. You've got to come to trust God completely before you realize just how powerful a mandate from God can be.

When you've been sexually, mentally, and emotionally abused in your past and your self-worth is at an all-time low, you can feel just as insignificant as Moses did when God was telling him to speak on His behalf, and he not only lacked the eloquence, but he stuttered when he spoke.

When you feel as if you're less than nothing because you've been put down and left behind, you'll struggle to understand just how you're going to get out of the mental rut that you're in. But, I've got good news for you! The same God that made it where seeds can go into the dirt and a flower will rise out of it and bloom with glory and beauty can do the same things in your life.

No matter who left you and made you feel like dirt, and no matter who put you down and told you that you will never amount to anything, they're not greater than the God that took a shepherd boy in David and made him a King. They're not greater than the God that took a church persecutor like Paul and made him the most prolific writer in The Bible.

They're not greater than the God that took a man like Moses, a murderer with a speech impediment, and caused him to lead over 600, 000 captives to freedom. You don't have to overcome any of your issues by yourself because God is willing and able to see you through all of it. You don't have to worry yourself about who walked away from you, because it is in fact God that has promised to never leave you and never forsake you.

Can anything good come from your brokenness? With God, nothing shall be impossible! If you need a self-esteem boost, God's got it. If you need a friend that sticks closer than any brother, one that won't abandon you, call on Jesus. If you don't believe that you can rise from the ashes of abuse with a testimony that can change someone else's life, I dare you to try Jesus.

Chapter 9

Pharaoh: Pain

If there's anything that can be associated with all of the Pharaohs covered in this book, it's the fact that pain comes with all of them. No matter what's discussed in this book before or after this chapter, pain is the common denominator. There is no level of bondage that is comfortable. We just learn to deal with the circumstances of captivity.

People often assume that the Christian life is one that's trouble free, but I'm here to tell you that it isn't so. Christians face many of the same problems that the unsaved face, it's just that we know where our help comes from and we've learned to carry our issues well. As I've often stated, we as Christian have to learn to walk with pain. We all have a weight on us, we just have to know how to carry it.

Pain is the great equalizer when it comes to the things covered in this book. No matter who you are or where you come from, if you're alive, you've experienced some level of pain. Whether it's physical or emotional, you can identify. The difference has always been in how we process it.

As we go forward into this chapter, we're going to discuss what I believe to be four common areas of pain, many of which we've all experienced. Some of you may very well be going through some of these issues right now and you don't know how you're going to endure. While the simple answer is "God is able", we want to give you more reassurance. We want you to know that God is not just able, but He's understanding. He knows what we go through, and even when the pain has come through a decision He's made in our lives, He won't leave us in despair.

1. Emotional

Emotional pain is difficult to navigate because we all handle things differently. What's a big deal to some may be a minor inconvenience to others. Things that some may take in stride might cause others to want to crawl into bed for a week. Much more than physical pain (which can at times become psychological), emotional pain can't be dealt with through surgery or pain medication. Emotional pain requires something beyond a physical fix.

We live in a time where people are confused about whether they should show people "tough love" and tell them to get over their emotional pain, or become overly sensitive to the point of coddling them. This world has grown more cynical *and* softer, all at the same time. So as people battle with their emotions, they often battle alone because we don't know how to approach things.

We're struggling these days with how we're dealing with those that are depressed. Suicide is still a major issue, and it's often missed because people are caught up in how things used to be handled. If there is anything that keeps us bound concerning emotional pain, it's those of us that insist on reminding people of what we "handled" in days past.

If we're really being honest, many of us that claim to have handled some emotional abuse and pain from our past didn't really handle anything. Many of us just learned how to function in the dysfunction that existed in our lives and in our heads. We may not have killed ourselves or even been committed, but that doesn't mean we didn't think about it and that doesn't mean that we didn't need therapy. Many of us just grew up with unchecked issues and untreated pain. Just because we survived doesn't mean we're alright.

Once we carried that pain into our adulthood, we transferred it to our children or others that we were charged with caring for. Telling people with anxiety issues to "toughen up", when it took an incredible amount of bravery just to leave the house today. Telling kids that "words don't hurt", when we still remember like it was yesterday being talked about and teased as children. Telling people what we endured "back in our day", when the reality is things were done like that back in our day because we didn't know better and had no idea about the psychological damage we were doing to one another.

As we've looked at this subject of being held captive by Pharaoh, we must know that no bondage is ever "successful" without some level of emotional pain and abuse being rendered. No matter how strong we are physically, if the mind can be broken, the body will follow. Honestly, so many people are carrying things mentally that we were never meant to carry. Doing that for too long is bound to wear you down, and if you're not careful, it will take you out.

While we know that there are many clinical names and diagnoses that we can give people with emotional issues and distresses, what we must acknowledge is that common decency can head off a lot of these things. Letting people know that they're loved before we assume that they're weak because they can't carry what we carry can help them before they ever need a doctor.

Here's what we know about Jesus and his dealing with people's pain: He was compassionate. He never made anybody feel less-than because they needed some extra help. It's true, there are a lot of issues that we have that simply start in the mind. It's true, there are some people that are overly emotional for no reason. There are some people that are dramatic just to get some sympathy. However, there are some people that literally need the help of others just to get through life.

There are some people that will get up every day and wonder whether or not they're going to take their own lives. There are people that are so deep into depression that they don't have the capacity to love themselves or anyone else. Some of these people are wives, husbands, mothers, fathers, grandparents, pastors, church leaders, and so on. They've been hit with some issues that's challenged them and even challenged their faith in God. That place between depression and giving up may be the darkest place in the human existence this side of hell.

We've gotta do better than just telling people to get up, brush themselves off, and try again. We've got to be willing to help them get up. We've got to be willing to brush them off ourselves. We've got to be willing to show them how to try again, instead of just telling them to do it. Prayer works, but there's nothing like an emotionally damaged person seeing your prayers in action.

2. Family

No matter how stable you feel your family is, there is bound to be some situations where family hurt rears its head. We've all heard of family arguments that have lasted years, and even decades. Not only have we heard of it, but many of us are living it right now. Sometimes a simple apology isn't enough to make things go back to normal, because often we're dealing with something deeper than just one incident. Just as it is with a debilitating physical injury, sometimes there's some therapy that's needed just to get back to some semblance of normalcy.

Family is often the most difficult kind of pain because that's supposed to be a safe haven. Your family is supposed to be that group of people that will never hurt you, and if they do, they should always be ready for reconciliation. It's through family pain that we find out that the people we're related to are often just like everyone else's relatives. They're capable of causing you great pain, while at the same time being incapable of a sincere apology. They're capable of betrayal, disingenuous behavior, and deliberate acts of emotional vandalism, without feeling any remorse. To sum it up, our family members are members of the human race, and hurting people that they're supposed to love is a part of their DNA as well.

I'd love to tell you that the pain that you experience in your family will always be reconciled, but that's not the case. It's not that God isn't able, it's just that we aren't always willing. There are people in our families that are completely fine dying with division. It's not God's plan, but then again, we don't always operate according to God's plan, do we?

We make it seem as if the pain that's caused by family is so much greater than the pain that's caused by others. That is, until we grow and come to understand what true family really is. When we consider the fact that Cain killed his own brother, we should come to an understanding that family isn't defined by the blood we claim to share (the truth of the matter is all of mankind are blood relatives, but that subject is for another time). The true measure of family is in how we treat one another.

Now, before there's any confusion about what I'm saying here, I understand what it means to be related, and I understand that even though mankind shares the same blood, we come from different tribes. But if you live long enough, you come to understand what it means to be family, and you also come to understand that some of the closest family that you'll ever have in life will often come from outside of your tribe.

Some people are caught up in putting a smile on everything and singing "kumbya" over everything, and that's all well and good, but it's not always realistic. Again, it's not that God doesn't want the family unit together, but if the people involved don't want to be together, we do more harm than good by trying to force it. We must accept the fact that some people that we're related to are in fact like Cain, and they're destined to be exiled from the family, for the good of the family.

We can't carry on as if the pain that exists in our families isn't quite often an inside job. Some people within the family don't want to adhere to the principles and the values of the family, and therefore, they really aren't family anymore. They're just relatives. Accepting the fact that some family will only be family from a distance isn't a sign that we don't love or haven't forgiven. It's often a sign of maturity and a sign that we respect one another's right to be who we wish to be, even if that means that we can't be together.

Romans 12:18 (NLT) tells us: "Do all that you can to live in peace with everyone". We can't get so "holy" that we start to think that the only way that we can do this is with joined hands. Some people, even family members, don't want to be bothered with one another because of some past hurt, and as much as everyone being together is desired, peace must be the goal above our desires. After all, there will never be any real reconciliation without first coming to peace.

I want it to be clear that I'm not suggesting or advocating the breaking up of the family or the ostracizing of anyone. What I am saying is that there are some things that happen in our families that cut so deep, that only time and separation can start the healing process. Forcing people to be with one another has only caused another level of resentment. Telling people that they have to get over their pain just because they're family is like putting a band aid on a gunshot wound. Depending on what happened, people may need time and space to heal.

Many of you reading these pages can recall some of the most horrible things ever done to you, and they were done at the hands of a family member. I've often stated that the reason family is so good at hurting one another is *because* they're family. They know those intimate things about you. They know *where* to stab you in the back. They know what secrets to tell in order to try and destroy you. They know how to kick you when you're down. What they do hurts because of the trust that you feel that you should have with them, because after all, there really can be no betrayal without trust being present first.

You can't overcome such things without prayer, but that prayer must be accompanied with your trust in God. I say that because people will often pray for a specific solution before they ask for God's solution. Sometimes, God will tell you to do all that you can to reconcile with a family member, and, quite honestly, sometimes God will tell you to leave certain family members alone. Not to hurt you, but to keep them from repeatedly hurting you. If God has to sometimes protect us from ourselves, what makes us think that He won't ever have to protect us from people that are related to us?

Again, we can't just keep pretending that evil is on the outside of our family because "we're a church family", or "we're a praying family", or "we're a family that loves The Lord". These are all the reasons that devil will attack your family from the inside, just to show you that it's possible. I do believe in having hope, but I also believe in being realistic and listening for God's voice. Be ready for reconciliation, yes. But also be ready to accept the fact that some bonds will be broken forever, and sometimes, that *is* God's plan for your family.

3. Death

In my 2016 book *Going Through to Get Through*, I did a chapter on death entitled "Going from death to life". The purpose of that chapter was to instill a level of faith in the reader that even in times of death, God is still God and there is healing after the death of a loved one. I wanted to stress the fact that it's the devil's desire that we stay in a place of "why God", and never get to a praise of "but God".

What I've noticed in my ministry and in the feedback from that chapter is not only are people still struggling with death itself, but they're also struggling with the symptoms of having someone die. It's the residue of the act. It's the pain that they carry much, much longer than the death.

Many of them don't even realize what's happening in their lives. Where they think they're mourning, they're actually just nursing their pain. They've become dependent on being hurt, so much so, that feeling good about life even becomes uncomfortable. Just as most people will feel out of sorts feeling pain, they feel out of sorts feeling pain free. The pain of loss becomes a necessary evil to them. Somewhere in their minds, they wanna feel better, but they're dominated by the thought that feeling better means that they're forgetting about the departed.

Being locked in this prison has even more negative connotations. While death does help us to focus on our own mortality, it isn't God's desire that we do so with fear, trepidation, and worry. Where God wants us to focus on our earthly mortality, He wants us doing it so that we can make the best of our time here. He doesn't want us looking toward the grave with fear, but rather, He wants us to do good while we can and when we can, because there will come an hour when no man can work.

Overcoming the pain of death is a matter of us looking at the value of life. I know this can be difficult, as some deaths are a direct result of the way the life was lived, but even in that, there's a lesson from God. James 4:13-17 tells us that tomorrow isn't promised to us and our lives are like a vapor that appears one day and disappears the next. The text, therefore, encourages us to do what we can, while we can. We can't do that if we insist on wallowing in the pain of a loved one passed. Know that they lived as much as God allowed, but you still have time left. What do you plan to do?

If we consider the fact that people that we love deeply will die 20, 30, 40, or even 50 years before we do, are we really under the impression that it is God's plan that we be trapped in pain for decades to come? There is still much work to do and much life to live. There is no such thing as pain that doesn't slow us down or debilitate us to a point. Why would God ever want a life of constant grief for you?

I know that we believe that carrying pain is a motivator, but I disagree. Good memories are more of a motivator than anything. Knowing that God can bring joy out of pain is more of a motivator than anything. Knowing that God has more for my life than tears and emotional distress is all the motivation I need to overcome what threatens to keep me down.

4. "Church" hurt

Now, the word church is in quotation marks for a reason. It's my belief that there's no such thing as "church hurt". The actual church has never hurt anyone, but people attending the church, acting outside of the true spirit of a body of believers, have hurt people. This is the type of pain that will give many a license to skip church, bash pastors, and give justification to why they don't support the church. It would all make sense if skipping church meant that you could skip people, but as long as there are people in the church, there will be someone there to hurt you.

As we discussed in *Are We Still Making Disciples*, there are people that come to church for everything but God. They come to gossip, they come to hear singing, they come out of habit, and quite honestly, some come to cause trouble. If there is a reason for hurt being in the church it has to be because people aren't there for the right reason.

For many, the answer is to switch churches, and sometimes that does work because some churches are more dysfunctional than others. But what must be understood is there are people that cause trouble for the church in every church. You're never going to escape that element of church that isn't about the true principles of the church. If you're looking for a church where you can fit in, it actually is the church with issues, because we all have our issues. Our best bet is to find a church that knows how to manage their issues.

What we also must guard against is assuming that all of the church issues are caused by someone else. While we do have people hurting people in the church, sometimes we have people retaliating against what was done to them. Not that seeking vengeance is correct, but people seeking vengeance is a reality. We can't complain about the pain that we feel in church when we're busy administering the pain.

Broken people will often try and break other people so that they're not alone in their pain. This is how a cycle of pain presents itself in the church, but we can't always just seek to expel people without first trying to help them. We can't say that the church is a hospital, and then get angry when we're seeing sick people week after week. Treatment must be made available to those that are hurting as well as those people that do harm. Once we do that, we may in fact find that those people are one in the same.

The way we overcome people hurting people in the church is to be sure that we're coming to church for the right reason. Our primary focus should be giving God praise. If we can be an example of what we expect to see in the church, just as bad behavior becomes contagious, so too can our good behavior. If we can keep God at the forefront of our reason for attendance, He'll no doubt come to the forefront of our behavior.

We must learn to identify the source of our pain, and this is especially true in the church. The church itself isn't the source, that's just where it happened. God is not your problem, because God has never caused anyone to leave the church. The devil is our true enemy, and sometimes he gets into the hearts and minds of the congregants. If we learn to properly identify the source of our pain, we can become better at treating and eradicating it.

Whatever is done within the walls of the sanctuary is done by the people. The pain, the hurt, the name calling, the lack of Christian love, the "me" syndrome (claiming a church that is actually God's by ownership), are all things that people do. We must first allow God to treat the symptoms within us, and then tell others where we got our healing.

Conclusion

Pain is a part of life, and there's nothing that can be written in these pages or the pages of any other book that can help you avoid it. However, I do hope to give you something that can help to alleviate some existing pain, and to navigate some that may be coming.

It's real simple to tell people to trust God and that God is a healer, and those things are all true. However, it's disingenuous to tell people that all they have to do is think on those things, and their issue just automatically goes away. Now, I'm a living witness that the more practice you get calling on God, the more confident you become in God, because He shows up time after time after time. But in order to know He's a healer, you've got to be in some discomfort.

When Paul mentions the thorn in his flesh in 2 Corinthians 12:7, he was speaking from a place of pain and discomfort. It's not specifically known what his issue was, but he was yet praying to God about it. He's reminded in Verse 9 that God's grace is all that he needs to endure any pain. That's comforting to know, but when people are in the storm, even when they know help is on the way, they still wanna know when that help will arrive.

When people are dealing with emotional issues, depression, death, folks in their family, or folks in their extended family at church, they don't wanna hear about God as much as they wanna see God in action. For the most part, it's not that they don't believe in God, it's just that they want the evidence. They want the pain to stop. They want healing.

God has in fact tapped some of us, just as He did Moses. God expects us to show some people the way out of their pain. God expects some of us to lead people to freedom. Some deliverance takes longer than others, but God expects those of us that He's chosen for the assignment to do our jobs.

We have to hold some people's hands, we have to cry with some people, we have to encourage some people, and yes, we have to teach some people to let go of some other people, some places, and some things, because some of them are actually hurting because of what they're holding on to, and not because of what happened or is happening to them.

We have to be willing to give them the benefit of our testimony. We have to show them what we survived. This bears repeating from Chapter 2 of this book: A testimony is about what happened, not what's happening. There's a difference between God bringing you through and God having brought you out. One is a process and the other is the completion of the process! We need to prove to people that we made it!

It's not about pitying them, nor is it about making them feel self-conscious. It's about showing them that they don't have to wallow in their pain because that's not God's plan for their lives. It's about letting them know that they shouldn't feel ashamed because their level of tolerance is lower than someone else's. It's about showing them that you love them enough to stand with them before their Pharaoh and demand freedom!

Chapter 10

Pharaoh: Spiritual anxiety (worry)

What are you worried about? Some of you may have a long list, some of you may have a short list, and praise God, some of you may not have a list at all. Whatever your current situation may be as you read these lines, you all have surely had some experience in worry. You've had the late, sleepless nights, not knowing how it will all come together. You've had the long days of pacing the floor, not really sure if you'll get the answer that you've been looking for. And, let's be honest, you've prayed some prayers while all the time wondering if God was too busy to respond.

I'd love to tell you that there's a level of Christianity that doesn't come with the anxiety that worry causes, but that's just not true. No matter how long you've been a soldier in the army of The Lord, no matter how long you've been on the battlefield, no matter how much Bible you know, there's something that can go wrong in your life somewhere that will trigger a moment of trepidation.

I'd love to tell you that saying that "The Lord will make a way somehow" will somehow cause you to fall right to sleep, but such isn't the case. When we're on a sea of worry, we're much like Peter. We'll see Jesus, walk towards Him on the water, but then take our eyes off of Him because we become aware of the storm we're in. All of a sudden, we go from mastering the seemingly impossible to drowning underneath it all.

What I love most about that story of Peter on the water with Jesus, however, is that short prayer that he prayed as he was sinking. He simply said "Lord, save me!" That's all he had to say, and Jesus went into action. Peter spoke more to Jesus' capabilities, not his own current condition. Somewhere deep inside him, he knew that Jesus was more than capable of changing things.

When we find ourselves in a place of worry, we need to have that same level of faith. Unfortunately, also like Peter, we don't call on God with the right amount of faith until we're actually sinking. We've got to understand that it's okay to call Jesus when we're on our way into the storm. Instead of calling Him in a panic, we need to call Him proactively.

As we move through this chapter, we will discuss the real source of our worry, what it does to us, and what it doesn't do for us. If you've ever read the 6th Chapter of Matthew, you know that Jesus addresses our propensity for worry and the disadvantages of not knowing just how much God cares for us. We'll look at a few of those verses and examine the advice and the reassurance that Jesus gives us in the face of those things that give us a moment of pause, when a moment of praise would be more beneficial.

Here are four things to consider as it relates to worry:

1. You can't serve Him if you don't trust Him

Hebrews 11:6 tells us that without faith, it is impossible to please God. What I gather from this Verse is that we can spend a lot of time overthinking what God said, when we could just be *doing* what God said. In our flesh, we have questions that we feel we need answers to, when the reality is, if God gave us the answers we were seeking, it would just lead to more questions. So in order for us to please God, we must trust God. And in order for us to carry out what He's asked us to do, we have to exercise faith.

If everything God asks you to do requires a second guess from you or a child-like "How come", nothing will ever get done. You will be constantly looking over your shoulder, wondering why God said what He said, knowing full well that you can't see as far as He can. Understand that God is not opposed to our questions, but when those questions cause us to stop working until we get answers, then we run into a problem.

In order to serve God the right way, you've got to be open to what it is that He has to say. Too often we like to tell God how to be God, but you can't be open to God with a list of demands in your hand. Being open to God requires that we put our demands to the side and be available to what He says. Now, let me be clear: God will hear your requests, and even grant some. It's your demands that must be put to the side. God is a God of order, but He isn't a God that's under orders.

Worry is the antithesis of Kingdom work. How are you gonna testify if you're unsure that God will work out your problems? How can you encourage someone when you don't have courage yourself? How can you effectively tell people to trust God when you're in a season where you don't trust Him? Let's be honest, believing in God isn't a simple proposition at times, and it's hard to go to work for a boss when you just aren't sure that payday is coming.

If you've ever worked for a boss that you didn't trust, you know just how difficult that can be. You're less likely to give your all without some assurances. You're less likely to go the extra mile here and there because you aren't sure that it will be acknowledged or appreciated. You don't know if you'll be thrown under the bus if things go wrong. Even if certain promises and guarantees have been made, you have to be willing to believe that the word given to you will be honored. If you don't have these assurances, it becomes almost impossible to give it your best.

So Kingdom work, just as it is on our secular jobs, can be hampered by external distraction if we allow it. If we're worried about our own stuff (which isn't really ours), we lose focus on God's stuff (which is everything). Understanding that all things belong to God will help us to focus on the task at hand. Whatever we're working on or have been given stewardship over belongs to God, and therefore, God is ultimately responsible.

Again, on your 9 to 5, at some point in the equation, your primary focus becomes your paycheck because, unless you own the company, what you're working on is not yours anyway. God doesn't mind that mentality out of us because it really is His Kingdom. We just need to work. We just need to release the burden of things that are beyond our control and do what we're asked to do.

Once we come to the understanding that God has never cheated us on the job, it becomes easier to exercise faith and it becomes easier to serve God. You no longer wonder about payday because you realize that not only have you been getting paid all along, but there have even been some bonuses along the way.

2. How far has worrying gotten you?

In Matthew 6:27 (NLT), Jesus asks us a pertinent question: "Can all your worries add a single moment to your life?" This has been a critical teaching point for me, not just when I'm teaching others, but for my own edification as well. When I sit back and think about it, worrying has never solved a problem, has never made a situation better, has never put money in my bank account, and has never improved a relationship in my life.

Literally, worrying has never done anything for me, but it has taken my peace away. Even for those that have worried and stressed over things to the point of actually getting up and doing something, you must understand that your action brought you something that worrying never did. And if God didn't move in your actions, your problem would remain. But worry has never done anything for us.

The stress that it adds to every situation is a distraction, a hindrance, and is bad for both our physical and our mental health. I understand thinking on some things, but there is a difference between thinking on some things and worrying about things. You're not getting bad news and *not* thinking about it. An overdue bill when you don't know where the money will come from, finding out that you or a relative is not in the best of health, learning that your kids have some issues that are out of your depth, or maybe finding out that your marriage is in trouble. You're not getting any of this news, or news like it, without giving it some thought.

You're fine just thinking. You're human just thinking. However, it's the dwelling on these things that will cause you to lose faith. It's the pondering instead of praying that will cause you to lose hope. It's trying to control some things that you couldn't even prevent from happening in the first place that will threaten your sanity. It's staying up all night when you claim to have faith in a God that never sleeps nor slumbers that's troublesome.

The answer to the question we asked at the beginning of this section is a simple one. How far has worrying gotten you? Not far at all. In fact, you've gotten nowhere. It may not have caused you to sink deeper into your problems and your issues, but it certainly made you feel as if you had. It takes an inconvenience and makes it feel like an impossibility. It turns a dilemma into desperation. As Jesus said, it doesn't add anything to your life. It comes just as another bill that's due, and you pay with your peace of mind.

I speak to you as someone that has some experience in worry. I've had those times where I didn't know which way was up. I had to learn that worry was never in any equation that led to a solution. I had to come to a place where I realized that worry will paralyze you. Worry will confuse you. It will cause you to stand still when action is required. It will cause you to act unnecessarily and irrationally, when all you had to do was stand still because your deliverance was on the way.

It's still true that God won't solve a problem that we haven't fully released to Him. This is the trick the enemy plays on us. He keeps us worrying because worry will cause us to pray without really believing that God will hear and answer. Worry won't do anything for us, but God can and will. When we succumb to our problems, we lose sight of the problem solving nature of God. Worry will throw you into a sea of "what if it doesn't work out" before you ever even realize that you were always standing on the shores of "God says it's gonna work out".

3. Have you forgotten how much He loves you?

In Matthew 6:30 (NLT), Jesus takes us a step further concerning worry: "And if God cares so wonderfully for wildflowers that are here today and thrown into the fire tomorrow, He will certainly care for you. Why do you have so little faith?"

And isn't that what our worry is really manifesting itself as? A lack of faith? It's so easy to say that God won't lead where He won't provide, or that God shall supply all of my needs, but why do we seem to forget that when it seems we're in trouble? Know that our faith in God isn't some one way street or dead end trail. We ought to put our faith in God because He really is a keeper and a provider. God doesn't just show up in our surplus, but He's even more present in our lacking seasons.

My suggestion to anyone that's in a season of worry that's hindering both their service and their praise is to always reflect. If you've ever sat in any class that I've taught, you know that I'll always ask this question when it comes to worry: "When was the last time that it didn't work out?"

Now, I always have to follow that with a clarifying statement: "Just because you didn't get your way, doesn't mean it didn't work out" (More on this later).

Jesus is making a point to mankind that we are God's prized possessions, flaws and all. He's making a point to us that God is in fact concerned about all of the details of our lives, both minor and major. The truest form of love is not just when someone is aware of the major things going on in your life, but it's in how they pay attention to the details. It's easy to make the assumption that God isn't listening when He doesn't move as soon as we find ourselves in trouble, but make no mistake about it, He cares (1 Peter 5:7).

What's often lost on us when we're looking to God for rescue is all of the things that aren't happening to us. We get so caught up on what God hasn't done, how He hasn't moved, and what we're waiting be released from, that we forget to glory in the fact that we're being kept in the midst of the storm. We lose sight of the fact that even as we're going through, God is in fact pulling us through. We're in a circumstance, but He's there with us, making sure that the damage isn't much worse. Whether we realize it or not, God not only has saving power, but He also has keeping power that is just as valuable.

If we're confused about anyone loving us, we shouldn't be confused about God loving us. Even as the theme of this book focuses on captivity and freedom, we must remember that for all of their captivity, the Children of Israel came out of their captivity with wealth that came from the hands of their captors. What that means is whatever it is that may have you bound in worry, God can not only bring you out, but He can bring you out more prosperous than you were when you went in. He can turn your worry into a windfall. Not necessarily a financial one, but definitely a beneficial one.

As we go through our seasons of worry, we should think back on those times when we thought we'd fail, but we succeeded. We should think on those times when we thought we'd never make it out alive, and we made it out unscathed. We should recall those times when we were faced with a Red Sea, and all of sudden, dry land appeared. God is faithful, even when we aren't. If nothing else gives us assurance that He loves us, that fact should.

4. All we've got is right now

In the conclusion of Matthew Chapter 6, Jesus reminds us of what we're actually working for: The Kingdom. He tells us in Verse 33 (NLT): "Seek The Kingdom of God above all else, and live righteously, and He will give you everything you need."

This is a reassuring word for any of us that may be bound by worry. God will give you all that you need! Philippians 4:19 tells us that He will do so "according to His riches in glory by Christ Jesus". Match that will Psalms 24:1 which tells us that "The Earth is The Lord's and the fullness thereof; The world, and they that dwell therein", and you see that everything that you need right now is already here, and God controls it all.

However, Jesus takes us even further away from worry. That is, if we're willing to go. He tells us in Matthew 6:34 (NLT): "So don't worry about tomorrow for tomorrow will bring its own worries. Today's trouble is enough for today."

Isn't that what's REALLY bothering us? Stop, and think about it. As much as we really believe that we're worried about right now, we're really not. What we're really worried about is what's gonna happen next. Even when you're in a tight spot, you're not thinking about right now, you're thinking about what comes next, and how you'll get out of it. Your thoughts aren't on your current state. Your thoughts are on your future state.

This is how the devil traps us in the "what if" and takes our minds off the "I AM". We get so focused on what's next that we forget to take care of what's right now. We get so focused on what appears to be dark days ahead that we forget that God is providing light right now. Jesus is looking to refocus us and take us out of a state of worry by reminding us that we have no idea what's waiting for us tomorrow, so our focus needs to be on today.

If we're really focused, we realize that, just as Jesus said, there's enough stuff going on today to keep us busy. By looking too far into the future and neglecting what we have to do right now, we often double, and maybe even triple the load that we have to carry. No doubt, God will help you to carry any load that you have, but taking care of today's things today can make tomorrow's load easier.

Often we'll ask someone how they're doing, and their response may be "Taking it one day at a time". I usually respond, "That's the only way God gives it to us, so we really have no choice". But there's wisdom in that response "Taking it one day at a time". As we can see, it's even scripturally sound. Taking things one day at a time is a measured way to do life. I understand that there are some things that we have to plan for, but we should do so out of a sense or preparedness, not worry. We should think ahead on the good things of life, not the things that give us stress.

All we've got is right now, and even that isn't as bad as we make it seem at times. However, I'm always encouraged to know that I serve a God that will be with me day by day. I'm encouraged to know that I don't have to wonder if He'll meet me down the road somewhere, because He's been walking this road with me all along. We've been going in the same direction all this time. He leads and I follow. I sometimes don't know where we're headed, but I trust my guide. I'm enjoying my "right now" moments with Him, and while I don't know what the future holds, I know who hold the future. And even more than that, I know who holds right now.

Conclusion

To reemphasize, worry is a tool of the devil. It takes us further into discomfort and further away from the promises of God. The Bible tells us in Hebrews 13:5 (NKJV) to "Let our conduct be without covetousness; be content with such things as you have. For He Himself has said 'I will never leave you nor forsake you'". God has promised to be a keeper and a provider, and the devil wants us to believe that He's broken His promise. The devil is, in fact, a liar.

False thinking and weak faith tells us that if God loves us, we'll never have trouble. True thinking and strong faith tells us that as long as we exist in this dying flesh, we'll have some good days and some bad days (Job 14:1-2). A perfect life on earth was undone in Eden, but a life with Christ became real because of Calvary. I don't know about you, but I refuse to let the devil make me believe that Jesus loved me enough to die on the cross and save my soul, but not enough to get me out of any other trouble.

So how do we overcome? One of the things that we must do is not confuse getting what we want with things working out. While at times things will work out exactly as we had hoped and prayed, there are times when it goes the other way. We must learn to trust God, no matter the outcome. We must believe that God can and will solve our problems His way, and His way is always the best way. It may not be according to our plan, but according to His, and that will in fact work out for our good.

Whatever we go through, we must know that even if God doesn't do as we requested, that has nothing to do with His ability and everything to do with His infinite wisdom. Whatever I'm in, God is over that too. Somewhere along the way, there's a blessing, a lesson, or both.

I encourage you, my brother and my sister, to hold out until God makes His move. Worrying doesn't motivate God, but prayer and righteous living does. Ask in faith, and God will answering in faithfulness. Don't look too far ahead because that's God's business. Sufficient for the day is its own trouble. You've got enough on your plate to keep you busy right now. Don't let the devil trap you in a negative "what if". When he says "what if it doesn't", you say "I AM is on my side"!

A Final Word

Don't forget to say "Thank you"

As we come to the close of this exercise in freedom, we should feel a sense of appreciation. Some of you have seen some things in this book that you have overcome, while others have seen some things that you're yet still fighting. It is my prayer that whatever side you're on, that one way or another, you've come to this conclusion: God is a deliverer!

In the midst of that deliverance, we must resist being ungrateful. God brings us out, but He never has to. As we've discussed in this book, some of our bondage is due to things that we've brought on ourselves. It would not be wrong of God to allow us to lie in the bed that we've made, and there are instances where He does that for a time. However, having that advocate that we have in Jesus Christ, we don't have to suffer eternally for what we've done. He pleads our case, and God shows mercy. For that reason, we ought to always have a "Thank you" in our spirit.

As we're coming out of bondage, we can't forget what happened in captivity. While there were some injustices and some things that were done to us that we wish we could've avoided, we must also remember that there's a residue on us. There are some ways and some habits that we picked up in bondage that are the work of our captors, but those ways and habits will also cause us to identify with our captors.

Just as it is with sin, when we have been a slave to it for so long, we drift into other areas of sin. The same is true with bondage. If we continue on with a slave mentality, we can go from one form of abuse to another. We're told in Romans 6:16 (NLT) that we "become the slave of whatever (we) choose to obey". We can either become a slave to ways and habits that lead to more captivity, or we can be a slave to righteous living, which is in fact liberty.

What to do in the meantime...

It's often more difficult for us after we've left Pharaoh's house than it was actually leaving. There's a certain level of comfort that we start to feel in captivity. We get so comfortable, that once we're free and things aren't immediately great on the other side, we start to feel the urge to turn back. We actually start to believe that we can reason with the thing that has oppressed us for so long.

Understand that there's a space between your captivity and your promise. This space isn't where God is dropping you off. It's where He prepares you for liftoff. You couldn't soar in your chains, nor can you do so in a desolate place. But you can soar in your promised land. You can soar once you allow

God to strip you of what was, in order to prepare you for what is to come.

Believe it or not, when the Children of Israel reached the other side of the Red Sea, they began to question God. After centuries in captivity and an escape that included crossing on dry land where a sea once was, these very same people not only began to doubt God, but they even made themselves a false god. For a moment, they celebrated God, but soon after, they mocked Him as if they had freed themselves. At a time where gratitude should've abounded, they seemed to quickly forget how far God had brought them. Are we really any different today?

As we find ourselves in what I like to call God's holding pattern, our minds shouldn't automatically shift to "What now, God?" What we should be doing in the meantime is reflecting on the rescue, while preparing for the promise. Know that God didn't pull you out so that you could remain the same, and He didn't pull you out so that you could go back to what you were. He pulled you out of captivity because what He has for you is greater than the things that were holding you back.

In the meantime, we ought to get a little bit closer to God. Where you once felt abandoned, He reminded you that He was always there. Where you once felt trapped, He provided a way out. For some of us, where we once felt as if no one could help us, He had already tapped someone to help lead us out of despair. During your wilderness moment, you ought to be trying to get closer to a God that loved you this much.

Something of vital importance to note is your wilderness experience will often take as long as it takes for you to get on the same page with God. If you remember the story, once outside of captivity, the Children of Israel wandered in their our personal captivity for 40 years, with many of the freed never living to see God's promise because of their lack of faith, lack of reverence, and disobedience. What that means for you and I is we don't have to wander as long as we think we do. If we learn to stay with the same God that delivered us from bondage, He's sure to deliver on His promise as well.

In the meantime, we need to take inventory of ourselves. What led me to be captive? What is it about me that insists on staying trapped in the past? What's in my mind that causes me to dwell on broken relationships, as opposed to moving forward? What's casing me to fear more than I exercise my faith? Why do I worry so much? Why do I carry so much pain? And honestly, why am I so self-destructive at times? Instead of spending so much time asking God why there's a holding pattern, we should be asking ourselves, am I really done with Pharaoh?

Don't look back

Something that I often mention when I'm in discussions on relationships is just because people broke up, it doesn't mean the relationship is over. As long as there's still a way to get in contact with one another, there's a way to get back to one another. If you haven't broken all ties and gotten rid of all methods of contact for a season, there's still a residue of a relationship.

If you know the story of the Children of Israel and their escape from Egypt, you'll know that they didn't just walk away, and that was the end of the story. The Bible tells us that Pharaoh's heart was hardened yet again, and he went after those that had been freed. So we need to know that Pharaoh might let us go for a moment, but that may not be the end of the story.

Just as God brings us out, we still need Him to protect us after we get out, and to keep us from turning back. I wish I could tell you that what you overcome will die out the first time you get past it, but that's not the case. Some addictions, some emotions, and some situations have a way of coming back after us, sometimes a little stronger and more aggressive than they were before. We don't just need God for freedom. We need Him to cover us from the re-attack of the enemy.

A fresh start means a clean slate. You may be out of the physical presence of your Pharaoh, but he's still on your mind, and you're on his. Remember, a breakup isn't final until all ties are severed for a season. Pharaoh is still in your thoughts. In your mind, it's just like that last argument before the breakup, and you still didn't say all that you wanted to say on your way out the door, but one more phone call ought to do it.

I'm here to tell you that once you're free physically, you've gotta take some time to get free mentally. That's what your wilderness is for. It's not to hold you up and it's not to get you stuck. It's to get you right. It's to get you ready. It's to get you forward thinking so that you'll never have to go back there again.

Takeaways from the book

Lastly, here are some things that I want you to take away from this book:

- **Name your Pharaoh!** – Don't pretend that nothing is holding you back, and once you realize what it is, name it. You can't even begin to fight an enemy that you're in denial about.
- **Know your God and know His power** – You can't defeat the enemy according to your own might. You not only need God on your side, but you need to know what He's capable of, and that He will show up.
- **Take ownership and be accountable** – One of the worst things that we can do is play the victim when

we're at fault. This causes repeat captivity because we're often going after the wrong Pharaoh. Sometimes YOU are holding you captive!

- **You can't free yourself** – Stop pretending that you can just think your way out of it. God is not too busy to come and see about you. When you're in bondage, you don't need an exit plan as much as you need someone to rescue you. God is the only one that can break the chains of your bondage in ways that they will stay broken.

- **There is a responsibility in freedom** – Get out and get better. Don't be the same person that you were when you went into captivity. God will often bring us out more prosperous than we were when we went in, even if that prosperity is in knowledge only. Don't squander your newfound wealth. Take greater care than you did before, so that you don't wind up back where you were.

- **If God made the promise, God will keep the promise** – You can't prove to people what God said, only He can, and He is sure to do it. He won't send you into anything without a plan for you to prosper. When you know the way, walk in it. When you don't, follow instructions until you see your pathway opening.

- **You are worth saving!** – Help is on the way! Be patient and keep trusting God. Even when it seems as if it's taking a long time for Him to show up, He hasn't abandoned you and He hasn't forgotten about you. Just remember: Israel was in Egypt for 430 years, but it only took God one night to get them out.

If you don't get anything else out of this book, know that Pharaohs come in all shapes, sizes, and forms. They're friends, they're family, they're fellow churchgoers, they're co-workers, they're internal, and they're external. Our chains can be placed on us by others, or they can be chains that we ourselves have put on. Whatever the Pharaoh is or wherever it came from, know that their entire purpose is to keep God's people from their predetermined destiny.

We have to resist the urge to play a part in our own captivity by living contrary to the call of God on our lives. Whatever it is that God has called you to do, there's a Pharaoh somewhere that wants you in bondage so that you never reach your destiny. But be encouraged, child of God. The Lord has bigger plans.

Even when we slip up and fall far short of what God had in mind for us, He's able to bring us back from the edge of destruction. Even as we're trapped into some things and it seems as if we're destined to be a life wasted, God is sending someone right now to lead us back to the promise. You can overcome Pharaoh, but you can't do it alone, and you can't do it with the same mentality that got you into bondage in the first place. You've got to think differently.

I pray that as we took this journey together, some chains fell off. I pray that a deliverer was dispatched to your location so that you might see the goodness and the faithfulness of God. I pray that you are patient as you wait on God to bring

Pharaoh into submission. And even as Pharaoh changes his mind and comes after you in effort to bring you back into captivity, I pray that you forge forward on dry land, as your enemies drown in the sea behind you.

It is indeed my fervent prayer that when you get to the other side, that you don't turn away from the God of your freedom and salvation. Don't use that time as a time of faithlessness and uncertainty. Instead, use that time as a time of preparation for the promise. Be encouraged, my brother. Be encouraged, my sister. Don't forget to say "Thank you". Pharaoh is dead!

About the author

Rev. Kelly R. Jackson has been an author/poet for over 30 years. He's self-published 9 previous works and has an online blog. He's a licensed minister of the Gospel, and currently a member of the Bethel Temple Missionary Baptist Church in Detroit, MI, under the leadership of Pastor Damon M. Moseley. He's also a husband, and the father of two sons. His work is filled with common sense, wisdom, spirituality, and humor.

He attended the Tennessee School of Religion for 3 years, where he studied Theology, Hermeneutics, Homiletics, Ministerial Ethics, and General Biblical Studies, receiving his certificates of completion in Phases 1, 2, and 3. He has also received his Christian Education Diploma from the National Baptist Convention Incorporated's Certificate of Progress Program (COPP).

He's an accomplished Sunday School and Bible Class instructor, and is the host of his own weekly radio broadcast, "Your Life with Purpose", which airs on WMKM 1440AM in Detroit, MI and WCVG 1320AM in Cincinnati, OH. He's also the creator and facilitator of a Christian marriage and relationships workshop, "Eden Principles: God's plan for love, marriage, and the family". For even more information on Rev. Kelly R. Jackson, visit his website at www.krjministries.org.

Books available from Kelly R. Jackson:

Are We Still Making Disciples?: Pushing the church beyond membership and Sunday Morning Worship
ISBN: 978-1541040182

Going Through to Get Through: Activating your faith during life's most trying times
ISBN: 9780692647769

The 30 Day Meditation: Acknowledging the provisions and protection of God
ISBN: 9781517606923

An Understanding with God: Developing a relationship with God on His terms
ISBN: 9781502341976

A Guide for Spiritual Living: Empowering and Uplifting Words of Wisdom, Vol. I
ISBN: 9780692333778

Temporarily Disconnected: A perspective on the decline of Black relationships and families (Revised 10 Year Anniversary Edition)
ISBN: 9780692675045

Peace In My Mind: The Journey to Find Ourselves While Embracing Who We Are
ISBN: 9781440134265

Scenes From The Blue Book: Poetry, Reflection, and the Spoken Mind
ISBN: 9780595449644

All titles are available for purchase at www.krjministries.org, Amazon.com, or wherever books are sold!

Made in the USA
Columbia, SC
27 February 2020